ETHICS, LIVING OR DEAD?

Joseph Anthony Amato, II

ETHICS, LIVING OR DEAD?
Themes in Contemporary Values

ROUSSEAU

MARX

DOSTOEVSKY

NIETZSCHE

ADAMS

MOUNIER

CAMUS

SARTRE

Venti Amati / Marshall, Minnesota

All rights reserved. No part of this publication may be reproduced or transmitted in any form or by any means, electronic or mechanical, including photocopy, recording, or any information storage and retrieval system, without permission in writing from the publisher.

Copyright © 1982 by Joseph Amato

Published in 1982 in the United States of America by

Portals Press
P.O. Box 1048
Tuscaloosa, Alabama 35403

Venti Amati
202 Park Street
Marshall, Minnesota 56258

ISBN: 0-916620-62-X

The text of this book was set in 10/12 Garth Graphic. The book was designed by Scott Perrizo and typeset by Karen Starkins at Westview Press, Boulder, Colorado.

Printed and bound in the United States of America

Contents

Preface ix

INTRODUCTION
Is Ethics Living? 1
   A World of Change, a World of Choice
   Progress, a Matter of Debate

CHAPTER ONE
Rousseau: The Creation of the Modern Individual 11
   Man, the Measure
   Rousseau, a Precious Heart
   Dissections of an Individual

CHAPTER TWO
Karl Marx: The Ethics of Revolution 25
   Mankind, the Greatest Good
   The Proletariat, the Ethical Essence of All Mankind
   The Labor Theory of Value, a Revolutionary Ethical
      Theory of Giving and Taking

CHAPTER THREE
Dostoevsky: Suffering Innocence, a Christian View
of the Good 35
   The Gift of Love
   Elemental Exchanges

CHAPTER FOUR
Friedrich Nietzsche: Beyond Good and Evil 53
   The Self Broken and the World Lost
   Egoism at Its Extreme

CHAPTER FIVE

Henry Adams: An Angry Patrician, Before Power
Beyond Measure..71
    A Patrician, Without Place or Loyalty
    The Measure of Events

CHAPTER SIX

Emmanuel Mounier: Personalism, a Christian Ethics
for Our Times..87

CHAPTER SEVEN

Albert Camus and Jean-Paul Sartre: Humanists in
an Inhuman Era...95
    Albert Camus, a Humanist's Resistance
    Jean-Paul Sartre, Ethical Experiments in Self-Definition
    Intellectuals and the Myth of Humanity

CONCLUSION

Is Ethics Dead?..111

Bio-Bibliographies...119

Dedication

To Catherine and Adam, who have made me part of the family;
to Steven Tonsor, A. William Salomone, and Don Martindale,
who joined me to a tradition;
to Ted, Dave, Mike, Maynard, and many students
who have meant community on this prairie.

Preface

For my introductory ethics course I found useful texts on ethics as a practical science, several decent introductions to various ethical systems, and a variety of historical anthologies of Western ethics. As useful as those three different approaches to ethics are, I wanted another type of work to supplement my introductory ethics course.

I wanted a work developed around the premise that contemporary man is in a unique historical situation. And this situation requires, I believe, a unique approach to ethics.

The work which I envisioned had to have a historical character. It had to consider contemporary humanity's changing ideals of self, happiness, and society as well as its altered conditions, increased knowledge, and broadened aspirations. However, what had to be avoided was a cultural history of the modern world, which would have no place in an introductory ethics course.

To find that desirable point between history and philosophy, I chose to write a series of short essays on selected modern thinkers. These essays take form around such major eighteenth and nineteenth century thinkers as Jean-Jacques Rousseau, Karl Marx, Feodor Dostoevsky, Friedrich Nietzsche, and Henry Adams, and such twentieth century intellectuals as Emmanuel Mounier, Jean-Paul Sartre, and Albert Camus. These essays develop themes found in their work, which suggest fundamental elements of our changing ethical horizons.

The commanding theme of this work, which joins these individual essays together, is the problematic ethical condition of contemporary man. At stake here are two questions: Is ethics living or dead? Can we define it for our times?

I discovered in the course of doing this work, that the matter of defining an ethics relevant to our times has been at play in all my writing. Despite my decade-long training as a cultural historian, I had not come to believe that truth is the daughter of time, that history subsumes philosophy.

In *Mounier and Maritain: A French Catholic Understanding of the Modern World* (University of Alabama Press, 1975) I asked whether Mounier's Personalism (which is conceded by most to be the fullest attempt to form a Catholic lay philosophy for our era) provided a doctrine for understanding, judging, and acting in the twentieth century. Mounier's Personalism sought to find a philosophy that transcends the individualisms and collectivisms which rule our era.

In *Guilt and Gratitude, A Study of Modern Conscience,* (Greenwood: Westport, Ct., 1982) I explored the roots of our divided conscience. With reference to a gratitude, which binds us to what has been given, and a form of guilt, which compels us to realize the good which could be, I seek to elucidate fundamental polarizations, which penetrate all levels of our private and public existence, a first step towards an authentic ethical consciousness in this era.

In my next two studies I intend to go further in defining the nature of an ethical understanding for our times. In *Pain: A Suffering Theory of Value,* my argument will be: our suffering (understood as the measure of our labor, pain, and grief) is one of our primary measures of the good. It determines the value of our work, sacrifice, and loyalty. By altering our notions of pain and suffering the modern world has necessitated an ethical reevaluation of the fundamental meaning of our existence.

In *Intimacy, Our Good,* I will explore the ethical implications of another fundamental transformation, the growth of individualism, privacy, and intimacy. These increased claims on behalf of the self have occurred, not by historical accident, at the same time as the collective aspects of modern society have also radically extended their control over the individual. The division between the intimate self, and the expanded state, established by increased bureaucracies and totalitarian ideologies, form a major, if not the fundamental, division between private and public goods.

This work, *Ethics, Living or Dead?,* joins my interest in philosophy and history. Its spirit is that of inquiry. Its intentions are pedagogic. It seeks to introduce students to essential terms, thinkers, and debates of contemporary ethics, and therefore, make ethics alive for them.

* * *

At this point it remains for me to express my gratitude to those who helped me with this book. My first thanks are always to my wife Cathy and my children Felice, Anthony, Adam, and Ethel, who always support and endure a book's long road to its publication.

I owe thanks of similar nature to my close colleagues, Michael Kopp and David Monge who generously sought to help me say what I mean, and Hugh Curtler, who has fully supported my teaching of Ethics.

Also, I would be remiss if I did not extend my special thanks to students who encouraged the creation of this work. On this count Kevin Stroup went way beyond the call of duty.

Dorothy Frisvold, our secretary, Laurine Fox, our paraprofessional, Shirley Carlson, Teresa Treinen, our student aides, have been indispensably helpful.

As always I have counted on the aid of our Word Processing Center, Duplicating Services, Academic Affairs, and my friend and master librarian, Don Olsen.

In conclusion, special thanks are owed to publisher James Travis of Portals Press, who has lent his encouragement and his Press to this project, and Scott Perrizo, typographer, of Westview Press, whose interest and skill has well guided this work on its final journey from manuscript to book.

—J.A.A.
Marshall, Minnesota
October, 1981

INTRODUCTION

Is Ethics Living?

THE PLACE OF ETHICS in philosophy has traditionally been identified by making an analogy between it and the other branches of philosophy. As metaphysics deals with being, epistemology with knowledge, logic with reasoning, and aesthetics with the beautiful, so ethics, it is analogized, is that branch of philosophy which deals with the good. Yet, however wonderfully this analogy seems to ferry us across vast realms of existence, it delivers us to the undefined territory of the good, territory where there is no fixed point of the good.

Our compass is immediately set spinning by questions: Is the good collective or individual? Does it somehow pertain to the freedom, will, motives, responsibility or action of the individual? The origin of the word ethics, which means character in Greek, points us in our search for the good in the direction of the individual. The whole Judaic-Christian inheritance makes individual conscience the most important reality. Even God Himself alters his Providence in response to the movement of human hearts.

Yet ethics cannot be reduced to the individual in the form of the self or the person. The origin of the individual's values and the consequences of his actions always reach beyond him. Dealing with the whole range of matters we consider to be morally right and wrong, ethics involves us with collective humanity. The good, as many philosophers over the ages have insisted, is profoundly connected to customs, values, and traditions as well as the justice, order, and harmony of a society. Thus ethics, at least in some of its discussions, invariably leads to politics, that branch of philosophy which, while focused on the nature of government, asks how, and to what end, do men and women rule themselves.

Ethics' presumption—a presumption it shares with all the other branches of philosophy—to discuss reality rationally, analytically, and systematically, does not place it on a solid terrain. In fact, its very commitment to analysis intensifies our awareness of how much dispute there is regarding the boundaries of ethics. Under ethics' inspiration we are led to ask perplexing questions: Is the good one or many? Where does the good reside: in the mind of God, the order of things, in the person's spirit, will, or actions? Is the good a matter of consequences, and if so, what sort of consequences, and for whom?

Attempts to escape the labyrinth of questions by identifying the good with a definite human end do not succeed. No answer provides us with an unbroken thread we can follow from beginning to end. For instance, once we equate the good with human happiness, we must ask what is happiness, whose happiness, and at what cost do we affirm happiness. Ethics gives no direct answer. Certainly it is no highway to action.

The more we study ethics, the more we simultaneously sense ourselves being led in two opposite directions. Each direction denies an autonomy to ethics. On the one hand, it seems that our ideas of the good and ethics are simply derived from our views of God, existence, humanity, and society. Ethics is only a specification of our philosophy of life, our world view. On the other hand, ethics seems always to be a matter of specifics: specific persons in specific situations, cultures, and historical periods, facing specific issues. The good is always embodied. It is thought, expressed, and acted out by particular men and women amidst specific circumstances.

In this study we refuse to reduce ethics to either the general or the particular. Instead, as if our intention were to embrace the extremes, we choose to join both the general and the universal issues to the particular, the biographical, and the historical. While we do not deny a kind of universality to all ethical thought and the ideas which compose it, we at the same time contend that there is such a reality as modern ethics. Modern ethics, we suggest, raises fundamental and traditional questions in specific and unique ways. Invariably, modern ethics' concerns revolve around the issues of the meaning of the individual person and a changing society. Among its most common questions are: What is the self? What is community? What is the self in community? What are the respective values of self and society in this radically changing world? These questions number among the most fundamental types of inquiry of modern ethical thought.

The major thinkers at the center of this study—Jean-Jacques Rousseau, Karl Marx, Feodor Dostoevsky, Friedrich Nietzsche, Henry Adams, Emmanuel Mounier, Albert Camus, and Jean-Paul Sartre—all testify to modern man's need to understand himself, his institutions, his individual and collective meaning in a changing world. Each of these thinkers confronted a world demanding definition and redefinition.

Rousseau, Nietzsche, and Sartre pursued the meaning of self. Rousseau sought self between the conflicting poles of individuals' happiness and community harmony. Nietzsche, who despised the emerging mass and national cultures of his era, sought to define the superman who would go beyond the values of his time. Sartre, who spent his younger years as a writer preoccupied with the meaning of self, served the progressive, collective causes of humanity during the second half of his life.

In two different centuries, in two different ways, Dostoevsky and Mounier sought to find the meaning of Christianity in a changing world. For Dostoevsky it led to a most severe reaction against all things modern. For him God alone was the source of the good; Christ alone provided the way. Contrary to Dostoevsky, Mounier sought to have his faith serve his times. In his Catholicism he sought the wisdom to understand the collapse of one civilization and the spiritual conditions of the erection of a new civilization.

Of the remaining three thinkers, Marx is by far the most optimistic. He believed that the eventual successful revolution of the working class would result in the liberation of all humanity. Inspired by the optimism of the early nineteenth century, Marx conceived humanity's liberation as including man's triumph over nature's evil and all social injustice. Adams, who wrote at the beginning of this century, shared no such optimism. In his bleak view, mankind had created forces it could no longer control. History was accelerating at ever greater speeds. It was running away from man, fating him to an unwanted future. Even more pessimistically, Camus, who experienced the Great Depression and the Second World War, asked how can man survive in a world inhabited by states and revolutions that commit mass murder in the name of humanity's betterment. Camus sought meaning and dignity in a world he understood to be absurd and violent.

No doubt each of these thinkers was profoundly occupied with ethical issues. How else could it be when they sought to give meaning and value to so many aspects of human experience in a radically changing world? At every turn, these thinkers confronted ethical questions of worth, value, and justice, as they sought to take measure of self, community, religion, state, and history. For them ethics was inescapable.

Upon this basis the reader might feel stymied before the task of suggesting any way in which ethics is dead. In fact, ethics would appear to be alive and thriving today, not just for such thinkers as these, but for all men and women who too must seek to value themselves in this mutable world. In this world everyone, in measure, is an ethical animal.

Our personal and public lives abound with ethical questions. Almost every major area of our national life, from the formulation of the annual national budget to another crisis in the Middle East, requires us to consider what is right. Almost every aspect of our private lives from the most intimate matter of friendship, marriage, or sexual practice, to the matters of business, education, and career, provokes considerable ethical considerations. From this situation one conclusion seems inescapably to follow: Insofar as ethics is inseparable from our consciousness of public and private lives, it could not possibly be dead. In fact, a more practical study could not be imagined.

To say that ethics is dead would seem not only to deny our situation as citizens of the most powerful nation in a changing world, but to contradict human experience. Let us first show this by starting with our consciousness itself. How could consciousness ever be separated from conscience?

Conscience comes with consciousness; judgment accompanies awareness. There are no perceptions of existence, self, other, or world which are disassociated from the categories of right and wrong, good and evil, fair and unfair, just and unjust, proper and improper. Our definition of self, others, and our relation to them, are moral constructions. We know ourselves and others in such moral forms as friends, enemies, debtors and creditors. Ethical judgments are indispensable to human understanding, explanation, and consciousness.

One proof of this can be found in the nature of human language itself. It is impossible to conceive of a human language that lacks the ability to issue commands, to define obligations and duties, which is without terms for praise or condemnation. Such a language simply cannot be imagined.

As our consciousness and language testify to the fundamental place of ethics in human experience, so too do the assumptions that guide us in our everyday life. Our daily actions rest upon ethical conceptions of the world. Blame, censure, punishment, and forgiveness occupy a great part of our conscious lives. Our commonplace conversations convey ever present moral judgments. Ethics, in one form or another, would seem to be among the primary human preoccupations.

The pervasive place of judgment in daily affairs reveals a fundamental assumption that structures human experience. We hold ourselves and others to be responsible for our actions. This is borne out, informally, by our gossip, opinions, confessions, eulogies, and plans, and formally, by our religions, politics, and law. Assuming that we are free agents, we use language, establish customs, articulate the law, and set forth moral codes. We constantly prescribe. Prescription itself assumes our freedom. Our notions of obedience and disobedience, success and failure, further illustrate the primary place we assign to freedom in human affairs. Freedom and responsibility put us before ethical choices.

It would seem that ethics arises out of human nature itself. Hence, the suggestion that ethics is dead would seem to imply that human nature has been fundamentally altered, and there exists a new mankind which conducts its affairs independent of conceptions, judgments, and disputes over right and wrong.

Even ethical relativists cannot deny the human preoccupation with matters of right and wrong. Moral judgments may vary from individual to individual, group to group, class to class, time to time, and culture to culture, but moral judging is itself universal. The diversity of cultures does not negate the prescriptive function of culture itself. Subtly with guilt and shame and bluntly with punishment, cultures value and order people's lives. Cultures apply ethical judgment to tradition, reflection, and religion, as well as to the most repetitive biological matters of eating, defecation, sleeping, and intercourse.

Ethics, consequently, would seem to be as vital as men and women are real. Ethical knowledge is a crucial form of self-knowledge.

A WORLD OF CHANGE, A WORLD OF CHOICE

We are our own makers—creations of our own definitions and judgments. We are our own ethical architects. We live amidst the variety of our ethical creations, which range from table manners to religious precepts, from diplomatic codes to the intricate norms of dating.

In our era we assume man to be his own maker and we debate universally all that man is. No realm, however traditional or intimate, escapes public discussion. We argue the worth of God, nature, and man. We always debate the fundamental boundaries of life itself. At almost all moments we participate in ethical worlds.

These debates are not just matters of abstract reflection. They give rise to organized groups, social organizations, mass parties and states. Literally, we fight wars over the good. Controversy over the good not only characterizes our era, but actually forms it.

Two themes convince us that controversy is at the center of our existence. First, change radically transforms all facets of our lives. This change questions our entire inheritance. It challenges our ways of both acting and believing. This challenge is compounded in our changing industrial society where no single commanding culture exists, but a variety of cultures (high, popular, ethnic, national, religious, scientific) compete to define the good.

Second, change makes choice, opinion, and debate our first heritage. This universal change (referred to as industrialization, urbanization, Europeanization, Westernization, modernization) penetrates everything. It alters beliefs, customs, and institutions once presumed to be as old as humanity itself. This change causes a constant revision of values. For instance the family has undergone a radical reexamination each generation. Political legitimacy and authority also have undergone intensive revision during the last two centuries. A steady improvement of the standard of living, a growing sense of equality, and a spreading belief in the right of each individual to achieve his potential, have formed the revolutionary credo of the middle and upper classes of the developed nations. And this credo is now spreading, with the most revolutionary effects, to the lower classes and undeveloped peoples of the world.

Global interdependence is one of the many profound consequences of this universal change. Global interdependence gives new poignancy to the question, Who are my brothers and sisters? Humanity can no longer be merely an abstraction. Humanity now has become all the people whom we affect and who affect us. Mankind has enclosed itself in a mutually shared future. This means that the common good must be rethought, and with that rethinking ethical questions abound: Are the goods of humanity and nation compatible? Should we now consider ourselves to be citizens of the world? If the interests of humanity are many, which of these interests do we serve? Is it humanity, present or future, which has the greatest claim to our responsibility? Do we owe future generations a legacy of nature? What right do we have to risk the conditions necessary for their very existence? These ethical questions are especially pressing in light of our present revolutions of population, consumption, production, technology, and weapons.

Change challenges the unity between the generations themselves. It calls into question the first moral precept of all traditional societies: "Honor thy father and mother!" It casts in doubt the entire old order by dictating a preference for future.

The old order has its authority in the patriarch. There was God in

Heaven, the king on his throne, the lord on his land, the man in his house. These patriarchs voiced the authority of an unchanging moral order. They counseled imitation; they denounced innovation. Old Master 'Ntoni, the old, wise, village, Sicilian patriarch of Giuseppe Verga's *La Malavolgia* says: "Be satisfied to do what your father did, or you'll come to no good."[1] This old order and its claims may survive in our hearts, creating a counter set of voices, but it no longer dominates the ways of the world.

For the first time in human history, future dominates past as the primary measure of the good. The corollaries of that revolution are: the new, not the aged, is the measure of the good; the young, not the old, constitute the ideal.

Wherever modernization is under way, awesome choices between the old way and the new way are faced. To what gifts are we most indebted? What do we cherish most, ancestor's traditions or present opportunities? How can we be loyal to both our parents' instructions and our children's possibilities? Allegiance to the old and allegiance to the new are not always compatible.

Between those often irreconcilable claims of past and future we must try to find value for ourselves in the present. Often we find ourselves uncomfortably sifting our meaning out of progress and nostalgia. Choices of career, marriage, children, property holdings and savings can make our minds battlegrounds for universal wars between change and tradition. Only those who have not been touched by the modern world (How few they are!), escape the dilemma of choice. For the vast majority of us there is choice, choice, and again choice.

PROGRESS, A MATTER OF DEBATE

The choices that engulf us in the contemporary era makes us conscious of the ethical contentions amidst which we live. If any one ideal gives value to our changing world, it is progress. Progress is the providence of modern man. As once God or fate (and the two were often taken to be one) were understood to comprehend the course of all things, now progress asserts that man is author of his own destiny. Progress promises happiness.

Progress' first believers were to be found among the elite of Western high culture. They alone could afford such a faith. But with the spread of commerce, science and technology in the seventeenth and eighteenth centuries, and veritable revolutions in agriculture, industry and democracy from the middle eighteenth century onwards, progress passed from the elite to the masses. Progress became the sustaining faith of the West in the nineteenth century and of the world in the twentieth century.

Progress was the faith that excited the energies of all classes and sponsored all the new scientific, industrial, social and political endeavors. The faith was compelling, not only because of the vision it offered, but because it brought the rudiments of earthly happiness. It meant more food, more warmth, more things, and a healthier and longer life during which one could enjoy them. It meant less suffering, less sickness and disease, less tedious work. Progress offered a way and a justification to escape the tyrannous old man: the father in the household, the lord in the village, the priest in the parish. Progress increasingly gave everyone the chance to be somebody. Progress carried the promise of getting out of the fields, having a career, obtaining education, and passing something better on to one's own children.

However progress as a faith fell on stony ground in this century. War and revolution tore the fabrics of national and international society. Totalitarianisms opened dark vistas on human cruelty. Some twentieth century critics have gone so far as to say that progress, along with the myth of a rational happy humanity, is dead.

That is an overstatement. However, progress, the most recent of faiths in the world, has already passed beyond its first age of confidence.

Progress remains a necessary belief. It gives an end, *a telos*, to the man-made change that encompasses us. It offers a purpose to the technology and the centralizing governments which engulf us. Progress gives worth to that vast exchange we make of the old way for the new way.

In effect, progress is a way of believing in an age of universal change. Progress offers a vision of the world we dare not do without. Progress is a kind of last moral foothold in a radically changing world. With it banished, what faith would sustain us?

This brings us to the consideration which will form the conclusion of this work: Ethics may be dead because we lack shared beliefs upon which we can establish a common ethical discourse. We lack fundamental agreements upon the worth of earthly and heavenly goods. We have no common culture that establishes first values. Ethics may be dead in an era of no first premises.

However, before we grapple with such matters as these, the discourses of our eight thinkers will reveal the making of the modern mind. And we will not err if we believe that their reflections on self, community, state, progress, and God, are our own. Minimally we share with them the perennial human task to give meaning to life, and the uniquely modern burden to find meaning in a radically changing world.

NOTES

1. George Foster, *Traditional Cultures and the Impact of Technological Change* (New York, 1962), 65.

CHAPTER ONE

Rousseau: The Creation of the Modern Individual

MAN, THE MEASURE

In the eighteenth century, a major ethical revolution occurred, marking the birth of modern man. The essence of the revolution lay in the declaration that humanity itself was the source of the good.

The cultural roots of this revolution are found in the Renaissance revival of classical humanism and its naturalistic vision of man, in the Reformation's new accent on conscience, and in the support the Scientific Revolution gave reason. Also in this same period of early modern history, transformations of the human material condition increasingly contributed to making human earthly happiness a possibility. Included among these transformations were an agricultural revolution which freed Western man from the law of scarcity, an urban revolution which gave the city the initiative in human affairs, and a commercial revolution that increasingly made Europe and the world part of one market. The convergence of these material factors and cultural premises explains why, for the first time in the eighteenth century, a significant sector of the West's literate population made man the measure.

This ethical revolution put man in place of God, nature, and tradition. It affirmed that man was capable of improving his own conditions. It rejected the notion that man's destiny was not his own, that he was subject to alien forces whose very workings left humanity permanently in a state of ignorance, helplessness, and misery. Humanity, this revolution declared, need no longer be the slave of family, church, or tradition.

Advocates of this humanism were part of an international elite, whose motto was *Sapere aude! Dare to Know!*[1] This favorite motto of German philosopher Immanuel Kant meant to him, as it did to his fellow eighteenth century philosophers: Follow the truth wherever it leads, regardless of consequences, even if it leads one into direct opposition to public and religious authorities. Indeed, even the loss of one's immortal soul could not be considered too high a price for the truth.

This humanistic faith also carried a belief in and a sense of responsibility for reform. From the middle of the eighteenth century onwards, all European institutions, technologies, and societies were subjected to the eye of the reformer. The reformer's intention was to make humanity productive, more orderly, and happier. The American Revolution and the French Revolution were the two greatest reform experiments in this era when government, knowledge, law, punishment, charity, transportation, production, business—everything was made an object of rational reform.

No philosophy better expressed the reforming side of this humanism than Jeremy Bentham's utilitarianism. Bentham, universal reformer, sought to create a natural ethics for man in society. His utilitarianism sought to reconcile individual happiness and the public good. "Let every man," Bentham counseled, "be the king of his own happiness, and only when these demanding, shameless and guiltless monarchs clash, or situation requires, need call for legislation, the highest principle of utility: The greatest good, for the greatest number!'" Élie Halévy reduced the entire structure of Bentham's utilitarianism to the two central points:

> First postulate: Pleasure and pain are susceptible of becoming objects of a calculus, and a rational and mathematical science of pleasure is possible. This is what we will call the rationalistic postulate of the Utilitarian doctrine. Second postulate: All the individuals who together make up society have an approximately equal capacity for happiness. This is what we will call the individualistic postulate of the Utilitarian doctrine. The value of Bentham's system is the value of these two postulates.[2]

Bentham's utilitarianism raises fundamental ethical questions. Is the good of one individual compatible with the good of another individual? Is the individual's good compatible with the collective good? Is man capable by nature of being rational, peaceful, and communal? How can man, who suffers and dies, make an earthly end his highest good?

Also, Bentham's system, like any other secular system, raises three other fundamental questions: Who is man—the individual person idealized, or future, collective mankind glorified? Second, what is happiness? Third, can happiness be collectivized? These questions confront every humanism which argues that somehow man is the highest good.

As no other eighteenth century philosopher, Jean-Jacques Rousseau (see Bio-Bibliography) reveals the range and the perplexity of humanistic ethics. More than any other thinker, Rousseau was the creator of the modern individual.

ROUSSEAU, A PRECIOUS HEART

To establish the primacy of humanity, one not only needed to assert the validity of human reason, but also to affirm the primary worth of human happiness. By the second half of the eighteenth century, many thinkers made human happiness their cause. Reflecting this sentiment, Diderot, philosopher, wrote: "Posterity is for the philosopher what the other world is for the religious."[3]

Like the sacred-hearted Christ, who suffers for all mankind, this new man would take upon himself the burdens of all men and women. Their happiness would matter to him more than anything else.

In that period happiness was given a range of public and private definitions. There were the public glories of intellectual achievement, social reform, and even revolution. There were also private images of happiness. Eighteenth century paintings show well-dressed people, sensuously at play in their well-kept gardens and commodious dwellings. In these paintings man is at peace with himself and his environment. Conscience — like the face of the smiling mother, the approving father, the true lover — looks on with full approbation. Consciousness and conscience are one. Innocence is perfect.

However, there was "a snake" in the eighteenth century garden of happiness. C. A. Behrens commented:

> They all assumed that happiness on earth was the ultimate good. This was an *idée fixe* in enlightened circles which seemed too obvious to need defense, and which involved denying both the Christian belief in purification through suffering and the belief of the privileged and militaristic societies in heroic virtues. [They] used the term, however, in two different senses which, as things were, prescribed contradictory courses of action. On the one hand, they commonly understood happiness as an individual state of mind, and, as Robert Mauzi has shown, they prided themselves on being the first generation to examine the conditions necessary to it in a scientific manner. But on the other hand, they continually spoke of the 'happiness of the people,' which, in the conditions of the eighteenth cen-

tury was connected with the idea of individual happiness only because it postulated the removal of certain obstacles to it.[4]

Of all the eighteenth century philosophers, no one so intently pursued happiness, and no one so revealingly failed to find it, as Jean-Jacques Rousseau.[5] He reveals, as few others do, the divisions of a humanistic ethics based on man's happiness.

There seemed to be two Rousseaus. There was that singular, solitary man, who throughout his life was without roots or home. This Rousseau never really knew his mother. He was abandoned when a child by his father. He was a perpetual wanderer who was not at home even with those who loved him. This Rousseau was a *déclassé* intellectual who, even when accepted and cared for by the "best" of his time (such as David Hume of Scotland), did not feel close to them, or respected by them. This Rousseau was a terrible burden to himself.

In the opening lines of his *Confessions*, this Rousseau sought to introduce himself to us:

> I have resolved on an enterprise which has no precedent, and which, once complete, will have no imitator. My purpose is to display to my kind a portrait in every way true to nature, and the man I shall portray will be myself.
>
> Simply myself. I know my own heart and understand my fellow man. But I am made unlike anyone I have ever met; I will even venture to say that I am like no one in the whole world. I may be no better, but at least I am different. Whether nature did well or ill in breaking the mold in which she formed me, is a question which can only be resolved after the reading of my book.[6]

There was another Rousseau. That one declared that only by having a place in a community could he be happy. This Rousseau, who always sought answers outside himself, temporarily converted to the church. There were the women whom he loved. They were often much older than he, promising to console, guide, and comfort him. There was the countryside—its fields, lakes, workers—into which he tried completely to dissolve himself. There were his constant idealizations of his own native city, Geneva. These idealizations, in turn, led him to praise Sparta, not Athens; to propose in his *Social Contract* (1762) a general will which would elevate human beings to the highest level of their nature. This Rousseau was no friend of individuality. He lived in hopes of the peace that community would bring.

Rousseau's pursuit of happiness, though often with great variety and subtlety, moved between the poles of the individual and the collective. Groethuysen remarked:

> His soul would have found peace and happiness if the world would have let him live according to his penchants, and his heart would have found satisfaction and happiness of another type . . . if he had lived a communal life. He would have been happy if he would have remained alone in some distant corner, far from men; he would have been happy if he had lived the active life of being citizen of Geneva. . . .[7]

This duality of ideals derived from Rousseau's life-long attempt to free himself from his shame and his guilt. Throughout his life he pursued, alternatively, successively, and even simultaneously, both *an outer world* where he would feel himself to be at home – no longer feeling himself to be the inferior, awkward, and vulnerable creature he sensed himself to be; and *an inner world* in which he would be free of the painful memories of wrongs he had done (such as turning his own children over to an orphanage; disgracefully lying and thereby causing a servant to lose her position), and those constant qualms of conscience he suffered over his "real" motivations.

Rousseau was a terrible burden to himself. He took himself seriously, even in his paradoxical quest to succeed in the most elevated circles in France and, at the same time, to be entirely free of them – especially the sense of inferiority they awoke in him.

Rousseau's destiny was to have a mind fully awake. His desire was to have a mind fully at peace. Peace, for Rousseau, meant to be free of judgment – judgment of self and judgment of other. How were they to be separated? Rousseau could not distinguish between the eye of conscience and the eye of the other. They both gave him no peace.

Rousseau's quest for peace was revealed in one of his very last writings, *Rêveries d'un promeneur solitaire* 1774 (*Musings of a Solitary Stroller*). Now almost without a friend, supported really only by his faithful Thèrése, Rousseau – in his middle sixties – lyrically sought to be at one with nature. Out among the working villagers, wandering aimlessly along secluded country paths, alone at the edge of a quiet lake – out in a boat upon its smooth waters; there, Rousseau would have us believe he was content. "There stretched at full length in the boat's bottom, with my eyes turned up to the sky, I let myself float slowly hither and thither as the water listed, sometimes for hours together; plunged in a thousand confused delicious musings which, though they had no fixed or constant object, were not the less on that account a hundred times dearer to me than all I had found sweetest in what they call the pleasures of life."[8] When for Rousseau those fleeting, frail feelings about the blissful innocence of the countryside vanished (as they always do) then the pain of self consciousness again entered the garden. Questioning, judging, and hurting, Jean-Jacques was forced to look elsewhere for his happiness.

Contrary to the *Rêveries*, a decade earlier in the *Social Contract*, Rousseau looked for peace in political community. It would provide not only a haven of unity for all who embraced it, but have a "general will" that would elevate individual wills to a higher collective morality and be, as such, a fuller expression of their humanity. In this community the citizens would not be divided in their alliances. Citizenship itself would make one ethical.

At other times Rousseau's search for happiness led him, as if trying to relive his own life, to theorize how a child should ideally be prepared to be an adult. In his classic *Émile* (1762), Rousseau's imaginary pupil, Émile, is left alone in nature to do his own learning. However, when required, he is deceived by his mentor, often in a most disingenuous manner, in order to be taught essential lessons about life. In his design of Émile's education, Rousseau contradictorily pursued the creation of a never-to-be person, who would be equipped to ward off the deceits of others, yet never have anything but a pure, human heart. Émile would see through custom and manners. He would never be confused about the true motivations of men. Like Jean-Jacques, his creator, he would have delicate inner antennae; but, unlike Jean-Jacques, he would be steeled by wit and wisdom to escape the hurt which shadows all human relations, especially for the sensitive person. In effect, Émile was Rousseau's revenge! Although he would be raised far away from the most sophisticated salons of Paris, Émile would, nevertheless, upon completion of his education, be able to enter into and instantaneously grasp the salon's most subtle strategies and the most deceitful games. If only in the literary guise of Émile, Jean-Jacques would have his vengeance against those who had caused him such humiliation.

Rousseau's search for wholeness took other forms. There was his love of Madame Warens (substitute mother, spiritual guide, then lover), his burning but sublimated love of Madame d'Houdetot, a supporter, a wife of a friend, and the real inspiration of the sensitive love he expressed in the *Nouvelle Heloïse* (1761). There was also his "Profession du foi" where he seeks a justification by conscience.

There he began with the proposition that only within the self can one find truth in a world which is a sea of opinion. In the self one attained true knowledge of God and the good. To the objection that so few hear God within themselves, Rousseau replied: "Conscience—that divine instinct, immortal and heavenly guide, certain guide of us limited and ignorant creatures—speaks the language of nature which everything conspires to cause us to forget. It is timid, it loves peace, to be on retreat; and the world and its noise frighten it."[9] As "the holiness of the Bible is an argument that speaks to my heart," so "the faith which God asks is that of the sincere heart."[10]

Rousseau never relented in his pursuit of peace, innocence, and righteousness, the conditions of his happiness. At the beginning of his *Confessions* (1770), he invited all mankind to come forth to stand in moral comparison. He challenged all to dare to ask whether any one of them were his equal in candor. Rousseau put himself at the crossroads of the world and called out to anyone to dare cast the first stone. At that spot, one which every sensitive individual today must pass, there stands Jean-Jacques—founder of the religion of the modern self. He is still heard to be imploring:

> Let the trumpet of the Day of Judgment sound when it will, I will present myself before the Sovereign Judge with this book in my hand. I will say boldly: "This is what I have done, what I have thought, what I was. I have told the good and the bad with equal frankness. I have neither omitted anything bad, nor interpolated anything good. If I have occasionally made use of some immaterial embellishments, this has only been in order to fill a gap caused by lack of memory. I may have assumed the truth of that which I knew might have been true, never of that which I knew to be false. I have shown myself as I was: mean and contemptible, good, high-minded, and sublime, according as I was one or the other. I have unveiled my inmost self even as Thou hast seen it, O Eternal Being. Gather round me the countless host of my fellow-men; let them hear my confessions, lament for my unworthiness, and blush for my imperfections. Then let each of them in turn reveal, with the same frankness, the secrets of his heart at the foot of the throne, and say, if he dare, *I was better than that man.*[11]

The *Confessions* were Rousseau's last attempt to find peace within himself. Thereafter, he was in full retreat until his death in 1778. His paranoia grew as the last decade of his life proceeded. Always sensitive to what the public was saying about him, Rousseau came to believe that all Europe was conspiring against him. In Rousseau's tormented mind, this conspiracy, initiated by fellow French philosophers and aided by David Hume and other luminaries, extended outward and reached throughout the whole of Europe. Kings and queens, city dwellers, newspaper readers—all literate Europe was party to the conspiracy. Its essence—one which "is so cruel and well organized that it is not even voiced"—was moral defamation. It suggested that Rousseau, author of such high principled ethical works, was in truth "a moral cadaver," "a moral monster," a person with a "soul of mud."

Rousseau described the effect of "the conspiracy" upon him:

> Cut off from the society of men; for me everything was to be shrouded in secrecy, mystery, and falsehood; I was to be made a stranger to society.... I was to be shut up as in a coffin.... I was not openly accused, arrested, or punished but a close watch was to be kept on me... and hatred of me was to be so carefully spread abroad.... this was not to prevent me from being treated like Sancho Panza.[12]

The phantoms of accusation gave him no peace. Rousseau felt himself to be judged guilty by invisible powers, and always under their constant surveillance: "The ceiling above my head has eyes, walls around me have ears.... I am hemmed about by watchful and malevolent spies."[13] This sense of persecution caused him acute psychic disintegration. The more virtuous he sought to make himself, the more insane he became. Naturally misunderstandings became more and more frequent; friendships became fewer and fewer. He believed his fellow men were beginning to hate him in return for the warm affection he felt for them. Rousseau reacted the only way he could, the only way he knew how—with words. He wrote another lengthy volume. It was revealingly titled *Rousseau, juge de Jean-Jacques.*

Made up of three lengthy dialogues about Rousseau's morality between characters named "Rousseau" and Francois, the work concludes with Francois' full assent to the following propositions: Rousseau is the author of all his works, and that his private life does not stand in contradiction to the high values of his work.

This work, *Rousseau, juge de Jean-Jacques,* failed, as the *Confessions* had, to quiet his mind. As the *Confessions* were written to end "his terrible embarrassment he felt in relation to himself," so the *Rousseau, juge de Jean-Jacques* was written to end the "terrible judgment" of others upon himself. Neither succeeded.

On December 24, 1776, he took the completed manuscript of the *Rousseau* to Notre Dame in order to place it on the altar for safekeeping. The gates were locked. He feared another conspiracy. He spent the night in terror. Finally, he convinced himself that God wanted to save his book. But this experience did not quiet him. He was not his own judge. Everyone else was his judge. The other had become the eye of his soul, his conscience. Ethics belonged to the world.

Shortly after completing the *Rousseau*, he took to randomly handing out a circular to passersby in the streets of Paris. It read:

> To every Frenchman who still loves justice and truth. Frenchmen! O nation once kind and gentle, what have you become? How you have changed towards an unfortunate foreigner who is alone and at your mercy. . . . Why must so public a scandal be an impenetrable mystery for me alone? Why so many machinations, ruses, betrayals, and falsehoods to hide the transgressor's crimes from himself when he must be better aware of them than anyone; if it is true that he has committed them? If, for reasons which are beyond me, you persist in depriving me of a right which has never been refused to any criminal, and have resolved to crowd the rest of my sad life with anguish, mockery, and shame, without allowing me to know why, without deigning to listen to my complaints, my reasons, my lamentations, and without even giving me leave to speak, my only defense will be to offer up to Heaven a heart which is without guile and hands innocent of all evil, asking that same Heaven not, O cruel people, that it should revenge me and punish you (Ah! may it rather keep you from all unhappiness and all error!) but that it should soon provide my old age with a more secure refuge where your attacks can affect me no longer.[14]

Ironically, like so many of his disciples in the following two centuries, despite a profound belief in his unique individuality, he had made the world at large, the very passerby in the streets, his judge. *His soul belonged to the very public world he despised.* The other, not the self, was the source of the good.

To a young lady who showed him attention during his last years he concluded a letter with these words: "Young woman, heed my words: whatever happens whatever fate is being prepared for me, when you have been given a full recital of my crimes, and have been shown striking evidence, and irrefutable proof of them, and have had their obviousness demonstrated to you, remember these three words with which I end my farewell: *I AM INNOCENT.*"[15]

DISSECTIONS OF AN INDIVIDUAL

Critics who have refused to accept Rousseau's challenge to confession have, nevertheless, judged him. Their judgments are based almost universally on the assumption that *Rousseau is the real father of all us moderns.*

For those who praise Rousseau and the modern self, it is his honesty which matters. Henri Pyre thoughtfully wrote: "A wholly sincere man? No, Rousseau never was one, and he never would have aroused such a passionate adoration if he had ever become that monster. But he went deeper and farther into understanding the value of sincerity, both to others and to himself, than anyone had done before."[16]

Ernst Cassirer judged Rousseau to be "truly revolutionary": "He *subordinated politics to the ethical imperative.*"[17] In Rousseau's own words, which Cassirer chose to quote: "The best possible government . . . is the form of government fitted to shape the most virtuous, the most enlightened, the wisest, and in short, the 'best' people, taking the word in its noblest meaning."[18] Cassirer saw the root of Rousseau's ethics to be his elevated notion of conscience. Again he quoted Rousseau:

> Conscience! Conscience! Divine instinct, immortal and celestial voice! Sure guide of a being ignorant and limited, yet intelligent and free! Infallible judge of good and evil, making men resemble God! From you comes the excellence of man's nature and the morality of his actions: without you, I feel nothing within myself that raises me above the beasts, except for the sorry privilege of straying from error to error, with the help of an intelligence without order and a reason without principle.[19]

Conscience for Rousseau, according to Cassirer, had its sole and highest purpose in the exercise of freedom. Rousseau took what was best in the Protestant tradition of freedom—and unleashing it of a dependence on scripture and faith—he, once and for all, made freedom fully a part of human experience. For him the deepest, indeed the only form of true self-experience, was the experience of the conscience. In fact, Cassirer believed it was Rousseau's conscience which Kant put at the center of his ethical system in the form of the autonomy of the individual good will. The highest principle of the good is the duty to do the good because it is the good.

In his *Three Reformers: Luther, Descartes, Rousseau* (1925), Catholic philosopher Jacques Maritain also agreed that Rousseau was the founder of modern conscience.[20] However, in diametrical opposition to Cassirer, Maritain argued that Rousseau prepared the way for the modern individualist's total egoism. Without clear notions of God, person, and nature, Rousseau left, in Maritain's opinion, no end around which man could order his thought. Anything which implied the need for self-reform—that is, moral growth and character development—was shunted aside by Rousseau. Inspiration and feeling were given primacy; will and conscience were swamped by impulse, emotion, and desire. Consciousness became formless. The self became everything and nothing.

Out of this conception of the self, according to Maritain, Rousseau formed a religion of the self. Everything that arose from the self was accepted as authentic and good. The intensity and abundance of man's feelings were made the measure of his human sincerity; sincerity constituted the reason for self-worship.

According to Maritain, Rousseau's new religion was Romanticism, which raised the self to primacy in the moral universe. In his criticisms Maritain was treading upon well-worn trails. In an influential piece of classical criticism, *Rousseau and Romanticism* (1919), Irving Babbit argued, "Rousseau became ashamed of being ashamed; he got rid of his guilt by blaming it on society. He initiated a reversal of tradition by establishing a new equation of worth: *je sens, donc je suis!* (I feel, therefore, I am), or translated into the familiar German romantic proposition, *Gefühl ist alles!* (Feeling is everything).[21] Rousseau also defined for an age so impressed by both science and tears, the *belle âme—l'âme sensible*, the tender, sympathetic heart. With their moral and rational senses shattered, Rousseau's Romantic followers traveled the paths of their sympathy, imagination, and then fantasy, from the love of woman, child, and peasant to darker and more menacing heroes, like Prometheus, Cain, and even Satan. If Babbitt is correct, an entire modern generation's romance with underworld heroes—brigands, robbers, rascals, vagabonds, and prostitutes—had its origins in Rousseau.

For critic Louis Brevold, Rousseau is an important link in the growth of the eighteenth century sensibility that turned against all traditional forms of Western conscience. Brevold wrote:

> We have now examined briefly the central ethical idea of four important representatives of the eighteenth century: Shaftesbury, Adam Smith, Hume, and Rousseau. It would seem justifiable to conclude that the sentimental ethics was a continuous development and that it was basically the same urge, however its expression varied from one writer to another. Shaftesbury's gentleman or man of taste, Hume's and Smith's man of sympathy and moral sense, the man of feeling of the novelists and dramatists, Rousseau's child of nature, all belong to the same family, as does also the beautiful soul, *die Schöne Seele*, of the Storm and Stress period in Germany. *Finally, a generation arrives which relies on rhapsody to raise it above the Ten Commandments, a*

> *generation which, after rejecting the idea of the moral judgment, puts its trust in the impulses of the human organism as the supreme guide to happiness and goodness.*[22]

The Marxist Hauser also judged Rousseau to be awesomely destructive. "The real originality of Rousseau consisted in his thesis, so monstrous in its implications for the humanism of the enlightenment, that the cultured man is degenerate and the whole history of civilization a betrayal of the original destination of mankind, that, therefore, the basic doctrine of the enlightenment, the belief in progress, turned out on closer examination to be a superstition."[23] Rousseau's followers, the Romantics, pushed their "individualism to extremes as a compensation for the materialism of the world and as a protection against hostility of the bourgeoisie and the philistines to the things of the mind."[24] Their proud identity, Hauser argued, was found in their negativity. To be against everything traditional — everything capable of being taught and learned — this was their glory, their heroism. "The system of intellectual values is enriched by a new category: the idea of youth as more creative than and intrinsically superior to age. This is a new idea, alien, above all to classicism, but to a certain extent all previous cultures."[25]

There is one point on which all of these critics of Rousseau agree: Rousseau's thought influenced the intellectual development of modern individualism, and hence Rousseau defined a significant part of modern ethics. The study of Rousseau's thought, therefore, puts before us fundamental questions that determine our conception of ethics.

To study Rousseau is to ask: What is the self? What is human happiness? What is human conscience? What is the place of feelings in morality? Or, to ask these questions in other terms: Is human happiness to be found in the private or the public world? Is the self unique or common? Does conscience most often serve the demands of an autonomous inner self, or does it reflect the influences of the surrounding world? Should our feelings be given an authenticity in defining the good, or should they be understood as antithetical to knowing the good?

No doubt these questions open up fundamental lines of ethical reflection. Without a conception of the self, all doctrines which speak of man as a moral agent or as an end fail.

The one question, above all others, which Rousseau leads us to ask, is whether mankind is constituted by separate, unique individuals, or by collectivities. The new humanism of the eighteenth century, which sought to make man the highest measure of the good, left a divided legacy as to what gives man his worth. His private or public self, his individual or collective existence, his temporal condition or universal possibility—these were opposite poles that entered into the definition of the new man who was to triumph over God, nature, and history. Needless to say, the issue of man as an individual self or as a collective being was not to be mute.

As Rousseau, above all others, gave birth to the *new individual*, so Karl Marx, the subject of our next chapter, defined man as an historical collectivity.

NOTES

1. For an excellent article examining the connection between free thought and cultural audacity, see Carlo Ginzberg, "High and Low: The Themes of Forbidden Knowledge in the Sixteenth and Seventeenth Centuries," *Past and Present*, 73 (Nov. 1976), 28-41.
2. Élie Halévy, *The Growth of Philosophical Radicalism* (Boston, 1955), 492.
3. Diderot, cited in Carl Becker's *Heavenly City of the Eighteenth Century Philosophers* (New Haven, 1932), 150.
4. Behrens, *The Ancien Régime* (London, 1967), 129-130.
5. For Rousseau's life and writings, see Bio-Bibliography.
6. Rousseau, *Confessions* (New York, n. d.), 3.
7. Bernard Groethuysen, *Rousseau* (Paris, 1949), 139-140.
8. Cited in Howard Hugo, ed., *The Portable Romantic Reader* (New York, 1957), 391.
9. Cited in Albert Schinz, ed. *Vie et oeuvres de J.-J. Rousseau* (New York, 1921), 300.
10. *Ibid.*, 304.
11. Rousseau, *Confessions*, 3.
12. Jean Guéhenno, *Jean-Jacques Rousseau*, 2 vols., (New York, 1966), II, 243-244.
13. *Ibid.*, 240.
14. *Ibid.*, 283.
15. *Ibid.*, 236.
16. Henri Peyre, "Rousseau, Sincerity, and Truth," *Literature and Sincerity* (New Haven, 1963), 109.
17. Ernst Cassirer, *The Question of Jean-Jacques Rousseau*, trans. and ed. Peter Gay (Bloomington, 1963, orig. German, 1933), 66.
18. *Ibid.*, 65.
19. *Ibid.*, 109.
20. Jacques Maritain, *Three Reformers: Luther, Descartes, Rousseau* (New York, 1928). esp. 93-163.

21. Irving Babbitt, *Rousseau and Romanticism* (New York, 1919), 142.
22. Louis Brevold, *The Natural History of Sensibility* (Detroit, 1962), 24-25. Emphasis is mine.
23. Arnold Hauser, *The Social History of Art*, trans. Stanley Godman (4 vols., New York, 1958), III, 74-75.
24. *Ibid.*, 129.
25. *Ibid.*

CHAPTER TWO

Karl Marx:
The Ethics of Revolution

THE EIGHTEENTH CENTURY FAITH in collective mankind as expressed by Karl Marx is the subject of this chapter.

Among the many ethical questions at issue here are whether the good is collective, whether the good is eternal or a matter of society, class, and history.

MANKIND, THE GREATEST GOOD

The French Revolution and the Industrial Revolution began that great transformation of the world that made mankind one by virtue of its mutual condition, shared history, and idealized future. These revolutions taught that mankind could and would change, that its earthly good was the highest good of all. Those revolutions gave birth to the social realities and political ideals of our time. In the first half of the nineteenth century, such fundamental terms as *industry*, *democracy*, *class*, *art*, and *culture* received their modern meanings. In addition, a host of new words entered our vocabulary, revealing the decisive epochal transformation of human experience and consciousness.

> Among the new words, for example, are ideology, intellectual, rationalism, scientist, humanitarian, utilitarian, romanticism, atomistic, bureaucracy, capitalism, collectivism, commercialism, communism, doctrinaire, equalitarian, liberalism, masses, mediaeval and mediaevalism, operative (noun), primitivism, proletariat (a new word for *mob*), socialism, unemployment, cranks, highbrow, isms, and pretentious. Among words which then acquired their now normal modern meanings are business (*trade*), common (*vulgar*), earnest (*derisive*), education and educational, getting-on, handmade, idealist (*visionary*), progress, rank-and-file (other than military), reformer and reformism, revolutionary and revolutionize, salary (as opposed to

wages), science (natural and physical sciences), speculator (financial), solidarity, strike and suburban (as a description of attitudes).[1]

These revolutions ignited a full and active faith in humanity. Philosopher Saint-Simon wrote in *The Reorganization of European Society:*

> The imagination of the poets placed the Golden Age at the dawn of the human race, amidst the ignorance and rudeness of primitive times. It is rather the Iron Age that should be banished there. *The Golden Age of Mankind is not behind, but before us; and it lies in the perfection of the social order; our fathers have not seen it, our children will one day reach it: it is for us to prepare their way.*[2]

This new faith had a messianic quality to it. It added passion to the eighteenth century's philanthropy. The new faith first commanded that one should open one's heart to all; one should have infinite sympathy for one's fellow man. This faith resonated throughout Western Europe, showing itself in the strength and diversity of political reform movements. Movements to abolish slavery, repeal serfdom, and improve the conditions of the insane, the imprisoned, and children, sprang up everywhere.

Social and national causes were expressed in terms of this universal humanitarianism. Italian patriot and perpetual revolutionist in exile, Giuseppe Mazzini (1805–1872), proclaimed the nineteenth century as the age of the arrival of nations. Nationality, he declared, is the role assigned by God to each people in the work of humanity. "The nation," Mazzini preached, "was a confraternity, sharing the same destiny, fulfilling a definite mission, welded into one by intense sentiments of love, devotion and pride. . . . The life of the people was a life of service, and its highest manifestation was the strenuous fulfillment of duty and self-sacrifice."[3] Historian-patriot-democrat Jules Michelet fused universal humanitarianism and democratic nationalism. He did not question the supreme value of France. "Look, my son, look: there is France; there is your native land! All this is like one man – with one soul and one heart. They would all die for a single man, and each one ought also to live and die for all."[4] Elsewhere he made clear his faith in France in similar terms. Yet the very ethical value which Michelet found in France was in its service to all mankind:

> We are not Romans of Tarsus, like the apostle to the Gentiles. We are the Romans of Rome, the Frenchmen of France. We are the sons of

those who have done the work of the world through the efforts of a heroic nationality, and founded for every nation the gospel of equality. Our fathers did not understand brotherhood in the sense of being a vague sympathy which induces one to accept and love everything, and which mixes, bastardizes, and confounds. They believed that brotherhood was not the blind hodgepodge of existences and characters, but much more the union of hearts. They preserved for themselves and for France the originality of devotion and of sacrifice which no one disputed with them; alone France watered with her blood [the Revolution] the tree that she planted.[5]

In this period, nationalists, democrats, socialists, all progressive and revolutionary forces were casting their ideas in terms of a universal historical humanism. Humanity was conceived as having an ultimate meaning within itself and its historical development.

Crucial ethical assumptions, which still shape our world, underly that view. First, man understood himself to be the source of all good and evil. He is, therefore, his own savior and destroyer. Second, historical development is understood to be more fundamental to human conscience than either natural law or revelation. Third, conscience is defined not by concepts of God and tradition, but by idealized visions of mankind's future. Possibilities are given greater value than precedents, or even present circumstances. All this meant that men and women, in profoundly new ways, had become responsible for one another.

Operating with these assumptions Auguste Comte (1798-1857), one of the fathers of modern sociology, declared that man had entered upon the third and final stage of his history.[6] In the first stage, the theological, man attributes power to supernatural forces; in the second stage, the metaphysical, he uses his reason and logic with abstraction; but in the third and final stage, the positive stage, man reaches his full maturity. He forms all sciences into a hierarchy. The highest study of all, man's science of himself, is sociology. It is sociology that permits man to bring unity not only to all human thought but to society as well.

Comte's contemporary, the German philosopher Georg Wilhelm Friedrich Hegel (1770-1831), also began with the captivating premise that all history consists of the equal advance of humanity and truth.[7] Hegel orchestrated a dramatic tale of the history of human consciousness. Hegel traced consciousness from its original differentiation from spirit, nature, and idea to its movement into human history, and finally to its specific historical embodiments in certain thinkers, peoples, heroes, and specific political communities. At the end of the historical process, consciousness supposedly returns to itself, having subsumed into itself the purposefulness, the awareness, experience, and freedom of all past history. History determines truth; it gives value and purpose to existence. Man, in the Hegelian scheme of things, in the end becomes God.

Of Hegel's many disciples, Ludwig Feuerbach (1804-1872) advocated the most advanced philosophy of man's redemption through self-actualization. In *The Essence of Christianity* (1841) Feuerbach dissolved God into human consciousness. "God," he wrote, "is the mirror of man."[8] Feuerbach argued that all the goods attributed to God were attributed to Him when man was in his minority. Now beyond such a state of weakness, fear, and ignorance, man, approaching his majority, can reclaim God's attributes for himself.

> Love conquers God. . . . For though there is also a self-interested love among men, still the true human love, which is alone worthy of this name, is that which impels the sacrifice of self to another. Who then is our Saviour and Redeemer? God or Love? Love; for God as God has not saved us, but Love, which transcends the difference between the divine and human personality. *As God has renounced himself out of love, so we, out of love, should renounce God*; for if we do not sacrifice God to love, *we sacrifice love to God*.[9]

THE PROLETARIAT, THE ETHICAL ESSENCE OF ALL MANKIND

To the new man, whom Hegel had given a philosophy of consciousness and Feuerbach a philosophy of liberation, Karl Marx (Hegel's most famous disciple) gave a will.

Marx was one of the secular Enlightenment's most militant children.[10] His ideals were derived from eighteenth century rationalism, as well as from French socialism and German idealism. His spirit was that of Prometheus bound to the rock, the romantic revolutionist at his barricade. God, Christ, and the saints, and all the religious sentiments of thanksgiving, sin, piety, humility, and repentance, were for Marx vestiges of the dark feudal order. What gave value to the world of Marx was human energy, consciousness, and action.

Marx believed that the emerging order of industrial capitalism would destroy all past orders of human production and give man a new relation to nature. It would liberate him from the toil, drudgery, fatalism, and all the rest of the pain and suffering associated with human servitude to nature. However, Marx argued the promise of the industrial revolution would not be realized as long as the capitalist commanded the mode of production. The capitalist subordinated the new industrial mode of production and all society to his interest. For Marx, the capitalist is both liberator and oppressor. On the one hand, he triumphs over nature; on the other, humanity must triumph over capitalism to achieve justice.

According to Marx, the capitalist's nemesis and humanity's liberator is bred right within the heart of industrial capitalism. It is the proletariat. As a class the proletariat, Marx maintained, suffers the worst abuses and injustices of the industrial new order. In fact, the proletarian is emptied of all past religious beliefs, family ties, and cultural traditions. In fact, all that remains for the proletarian is the revolutionary awareness that he had lost everything; yet he, the majority, can retake everything.

Like Hegel's, Marx's view of existence was a historical view of human development. As Hegel stressed consciousness, Marx focused on human productive powers. "The Proletariat for Marx," according to Karl Löwith,

> is a society which has an absolute duty because of its absolute opposition to the existing order. Only the proletariat, the complete privation of humanity, is capable of achieving once more the unity and completeness of man. It is from this exception to bourgeois society that Marx creates his ideal of a new, universal man, purely human.[11]

To Marx, the proletariat's struggle involved more than class against class. It carried all man's desires since time immemorial to control his own destiny. In Marx's idealization, the proletariat

> has a universal character because of its universal sufferings and lays claim to no particular right, because it is the object of no particular injustice, but of injustice in general. This class can no longer lay claim to a historical status, but only to a human one. It is finally, a sphere that cannot emancipate itself without emancipating these other spheres themselves. In a word, it is the complete loss of humanity and thus can only recover itself by a complete redemption of humanity.[12]

According to Marx, the proletariat is a new species of mankind. Like a Prometheus off his rock, proletarian man commands all his energy, intelligence, imagination, and potential. He is free of past myths, moralities, and values; he is free of class interest, individuality and selfishness. For Marx, the proletariat transcends the divisions between the private and public spheres of life. At last the proletariat is free and the world is open. Marx wrote of this imagined emancipation, "the real, individual man has absorbed into himself the abstract citizen; when as an individual man, in his everyday life, in his work, and in his relationships, he has become a *species-being*."[13] He "has recognized and organized his own powers (*forces-propres*) and social powers so that he no longer separates this social power from himself as political power."[14]

What Dostoevsky and religious reactionaries most rallied against, Marx proclaimed as an ideal: Man attains man. He exists *by*, and *for*, himself alone. Banished forever are not only the ruling classes and their religion, but even the source of religion itself, which for Marx arose from a heartless world and soulless circumstances.

Marx preached rebellion. "The categorical principle," he proclaimed, "is to overthrow all circumstances in which man is humiliated, enslaved, abandoned, and disposed."[15] Marx made the idealized man of tomorrow the measure of everything past and present. The idealized man, for Marx, justified revolution, and gives the ethical right of one class to liquidate another.

Simultaneously conceiving the proletariat's victory as both inevitable and heroic, Marx equipped the revolutionist for action with dual ethical justification. On the one hand, his actions are sanctioned by history, by all that is necessary. On the other hand, the revolutionist takes to him all rights of heroism, freedom, great will, self-sacrifice, and yet other values which surround those who martyr themselves for the higher good. Furthermore, for Marx, his conscience must be shaped by today's realities and tomorrow's possibilities. His revolutionary discipleship cannot be limited by private debts or personal passions. Like a Christian before his suffering Christ, the revolutionist must forever seek focus on humanity as reality and possibility.

Marx's philosophy has flourished for many reasons. First it carries within itself the most profound aspirations of the Enlightenment, of rationalism, and of universalism. Second, to an unrivaled degree Marxism fuses explanations of the French Revolution and the Industrial Revolution into a single theory; that is, it joins the notions of revolution as something abrupt and violent to those of revolution as something gradual, evolutionary, and total. Third, all change—be it technological adaptation, institutional mutation, spontaneous uprising, wars, etc. — is made a part of the eventual victory and fulfillment of humanity. Optimism is at the heart of Marx's philosophy. Today's sacrifices are given a purpose. If only vicariously — that is through one's children — happiness was finally conceived to be attainable upon this earth.

Marxism appeals especially to intellectuals. It is among the most ecumenical of secular faiths. It allows intellectuals to claim to understand and to transcend the public life; to survey the course of nations and classes at large; to pontificate on mankind's past, present, and future; to declare themselves to be social theorists, moralists, and activists. In Marxist theory they also find a language to vent the most petty resentments about their inferior place in the order of things, as well as articulate the most grandiose presumptions about their role as being the martyr-savior of the downtrodden. Marxism allows a connection between them and great causes; it permits the pride of subtlety and expertise. It is also a knowledge which permits entrance into the priesthood of radical intellectuals. At the same time it furnishes ties to a great revolutionary tradition, while dissociating one from the crimes of the ruling classes.

Furthermore, Marxism offers fundamental insights into the exchanges of modern society. At the same time, it raises fundamental questions about reciprocity in modern society: Who does what to whom, and why?

THE LABOR THEORY OF VALUE, A REVOLUTIONARY ETHICAL THEORY OF GIVING AND TAKING

No one rivaled Marx in formulating the new aspirations and the new contradictions of the industrial world into a single system.[16] His work is a monumental attempt to value human *giving and taking* in the industrial world.

Marx placed action at the center of human existence. Man's foremost action was the mode of production (his manner of producing his wealth), which in turn determines his relationship to nature. The Industrial Revolution, Marx contended, put human action on a new plane of existence. With industry man no longer needed to assume scarcity and misery to be his natural condition. Industry meant, Marx argued (like Feuerbach), that man's minority was over. Man no longer needed to look to God; existence was now for man to understand and control. Man could become his own provider, as well as his own source of knowledge, good, and justice. Hence, the Industrial Revolution was for Marx the beginning of humanity's passage from God to man, from necessity to freedom, from nature to history.

For Marx the Industrial Revolution was initiated by capitalists who brought together machine and labor, not to liberate man, but to make profit. To the interaction of machine (which represented the new knowledge and power) and labor, Marx joined a scientific and an ethical understanding of the Industrial Revolution. Adopting a labor theory of value, Marx argued that labor—not nature, land, or other gifts of God, scarcity, ingenuity, or control—was the source of human wealth.

Marx adopted a labor theory of value, and gave it a variety of meanings. As a technical theory it was used in *Das Kapital* (1885) to mean: "The fact that a commodity is a value means that it is materialized abstract labor, or, in other terms, that it has absorbed a part of the total wealth-producing activity of society."[17] On a more elemental level, Marx spoke of the labor theory of value as if it pertained to all the suffering (misery, pain, struggle) which men must endure to make a living, as well as all the energy, reason, and imagination they must sacrifice to earn their wages.

Marx predicted that this exploitation would lead to universal revolution. This revolution would produce a new order of mankind. The agent of this revolution would be the proletariat. For Marx, as we have seen, the proletariat embodied not just the promise of his own future but all humanity's future.

The capitalist order, Marx contended in his 1844 *Manuscripts*, had reduced the proletariat to the level of a commodity. "The worker becomes," as he is destined to become in the capitalist order, "a cheaper commodity the more he produces."[18] His work becomes alien and external to him. It is not a means to his well being, but the very condition of his misery—and oppression. The proletariat, however, has no choice but to work. Marx wrote in *Wage Labour and Capital* (1849):

> Labour is the worker's own life-activity.... And this life-activity he sells to another person in order to secure the necessary *means of subsistence*. Thus his life activity is for him only a means to enable him to exist. He works in order to live. He does not ever reckon labour as part of his life, it is rather a *sacrifice of his life*.[19]

The proletariat's labor, thus, is inimical to himself. He works against his own nature; that is, to use the abstract language of the *Manuscripts*, alienated labor reverses human essence and existence: man, labor, life activity and his *essence*, are reduced to being only a means for *existence*.

On an ethical plane, Marx was arguing that everything has been stolen from the worker. His life has been purchased by wages. His surplus labor (that portion of labor which goes beyond the labor embodied in the subsistence goods he receives in exchange for his labor) has been stolen for profit. Individually and collectively, he becomes an empty vessel. The proletariat's entire past is negated. However, what remains for him (like Hegel's slave), is a potential consciousness that all has been taken from him and that everything should be returned to him.

Suffering all the contradictions of capitalist society, the conscious proletariat comes to act for all mankind. The proletariat's struggle, for Marx, is far more than a class struggle. The proletariat does not have a particular goal but a universal one. In Marx's words, "the proletariat is the complete loss of humanity and thus can only recover itself by a complete redemption of humanity."[20]

For Marx, the proletarian is, by virtue of his alienation and the nature of his reclamation, nothing other than "a new species of mankind."[21] This victory means that the new human powers of the Industrial Revolution will be put in the service of man. Human labor would be used only for, not against, man; classes would no longer exist; distinctions between the material and the spiritual, the immanent and the transcendent, the public and private, would disappear. With the revolution *man attains man.*

Marx's thought was a profound testimony on behalf of human happiness. Marx believed in the ultimate compatibility between individual man and technological progress and happiness, revolution and social justice. This optimism accounts for the appeal of Marx's thought. Since the last third of the nineteenth century his thought has flourished throughout the developed and underdeveloped world, inspiring individual intellectuals, forming schools both orthodox and reformist, supplying revolutionists with their banners and states with the principles of their legitimacy and authority. It carries within itself the most profound claims of Enlightenment rationalism to order existence and the redemptive aspirations of Social Romanticism to save humanity.

Marx's optimism also won him critics. Among his most severe critics was Dostoevsky. Man, by himself, according to Dostoevsky, would never find justice, happiness, and peace. Whereas Marx said that the good is of man and his labor, Dostoevsky contended that the good is of God and his Grace.

NOTES

1. Raymond Williams, *Culture and Society, 1789-1950* (New York, 1966), XV.
2. Cited in Renato Poggioli's *The Oaten Flute* (Cambridge, Mass., 1975), 9.
3. Cited in J. L. Talmon, *Romanticism and Revolt, Europe 1815-1848* (New York, 1967), 116-117.
4. Jules Michelet, *The People* (Chicago, 1973), 204.
5. *Ibid.*, 185.
6. In his *Prophets of Paris* (New York, 1962), Frank Manuel remarked: "Comte abandoned the idea and name of God for a love of humanity so general that it led to a total absorption in the Great Being," 309. Manuel concluded that Comte as well as Turgot, Condorcet, Saint-Simon, and Fourier, failed "to contemplate the inherently tragic aspects of life itself, beyond the consolation of philosophy and history, that reduces humanity to their philanthropy," 315.
7. For one brief introduction to Hegel see Frederick G. Weiss, ed., *Hegel, the Essential Writings* (New York, 1974).
8. Ludwig Feuerbach, *The Essence of Christianity* (Trans. George Eliot) (New York, 1957), 63.
9. *Ibid.*, 53.
10. For works by and about Marx and his times, see the Bio-Bibliography.
11. Karl Löwith, *From Hegel to Nietzsche. The Revolution in Nineteenth Century Thought* (New York, 1964), 315.
12. Cited in David McLellan, *Karl Marx* (New York, 1975), 28-29.
13. *Ibid.*, 27.
14. *Ibid.*
15. *Ibid.*, 28.
16. A broad historicist approach to Marx's thought is offered by George Lichtheim's *Marxism, An Historical and Critical Study* (New York, 1961).
17. Paul Sweezy, *The Theory of Capitalist Development. Principles of Marxian Political Development* (New York, 1942), 33.
18. *Economic and Philosophic Manuscripts* (1844), in Loyd Easton and Kurt Guddat, eds., *Writings of the Young Marx* (Garden City, N.Y., 1967), 289.
19. Shlomo Avineri, *The Social and Political Thought of Karl Marx* (Cambridge, England, 1968), 107.
20. McLellan, 28-29.
21. *Ibid.*, 27.

CHAPTER THREE

Dostoevsky: Suffering Innocence, A Christian View of the Good

WHAT IS THE SOURCE of the good? Is the good given, or is it earned? If it is given, who or what gives it? If it is earned, how is it earned, by intelligence, will, suffering, or work? And if the good is possessed, how is it held: as a possession, a virtue, or a grace? Is the good subject to human control?

In answering these very first questions of ethics, those pertaining to the source and nature of the good, Dostoevsky saw God, His grace, and human suffering and love as the essential sources of the good.[1] This spiritual view set Feodor Dostoevsky (1821–1881) in profound opposition to the progressive views of his era and was the source of Dostoevsky's conscious opposition to secular historical humanists like Karl Marx.

As Marx wrote of the earthly triumph of humanity, so Dostoevsky wrote of mankind's spiritual suffering. As Marx thought of mankind surpassing God, so Dostoevsky advocated its need to return to God. As Marx looked to revolution for man's answer, so Dostoevsky looked to forgiveness.

The young Dostoevsky shared many of the sentiments and assumptions which gave rise to Marxism. He had imbibed the fashionable sensibilities of pre-1848 Europe. Influenced by Social Romanticism, he lent, so to speak, his heart to all the downtrodden, to "the insulted and the injured," to use the title of one of his early works. The young Dostoevsky belonged to a small, progressive, and, from the point of view of the reactionary government of Nicholas I, dangerously radical circle. In fact, in 1849, because of his membership in the Petrashevsky Circle, Dostoevsky was arrested, judged guilty, and sentenced to death. He was spared that fate only at the very last moment by the Tsar—whose mercy was surpassed by his love of the theatrical. Just before the execution took place, a messenger from the Tsar arrived, announcing the commutation of the sentence. Dostoevsky would be banished to Siberia.

The mature Dostoevsky who returned from a lengthy stay in Siberia was a changed man. His liberal views were gone. In *Notes from the Underground* (1864), the first truly significant piece he wrote after his banishment, Dostoevsky mounted a full scale attack against the progressive, secular values of the West. Dostoevsky now denied the fundamental progressive assumption that man was capable of either knowing or doing the good. Dostoevsky believed that the presumption to know and to do the good, separate from God, was sinful. And pride, Dostoevsky believed, not only separates man from God but subjects him to possession by Satan.

As one side of Dostoevsky's literary work was dedicated to the exploration of sin – especially the sin of intellectual pride – the other side was the search for redemption. Dostoevsky found the way of redemption in pride's antithesis, pious gratitude to God. For Dostoevsky, man's moral sense must start with the realization that the good is God-given. He must acknowledge the gifts of God which are not only the fundamental acts of Creation, the Incarnation, and the Resurrection, but the gifts of wisdom, love, and hope that come to man. Wisdom, for Dostoevsky, is found in the cross.

Dostoevsky joined love and wisdom together in the characters of the humble, innocent persons. These characters, modelled after the suffering Christ, confront the strong-willed, proud individual with the gift of love. The drama turns on the acceptance or the rejection of love. The testing gift of innocent love forms the plots of Dostoevsky's major novels, *The Idiot* (1868-1869), *The Possessed* (1871-1872), and *The Brothers Karamazov* (1879-1880). This theme had already been given form by Dostoevsky in his first major and best known novel, *Crime and Punishment* (1866). It is this novel which we now examine.

THE GIFT OF LOVE

Raskolnikov is the protagonist of *Crime and Punishment*. He is by far the best known of Dostoevsky's underground heroes. He murdered because he could not accept a gift of love, and he was restored by a gift of love he did accept.

Like so many of the student intellectuals of the era, the Raskolnikov whom we meet on the opening pages of *Crime and Punishment* lived among the urban poor. However, unlike the poor, it was pride that bid him to care less and less about making a living. He had stopped tutoring. He became more and more reluctant to do translations procured for him by his friend, Razumikhin. He had no other friends.

Inspired by romantic literature, Dostoevsky set Raskolnikov apart from the rest of mankind. For him there were only the streets, the pubs and the restaurants of St. Petersburg, and his small attic room with its desk, chair, and bed. He was a spider in his web, to use a metaphor with which Dostoevsky often described his evil, brooding characters. Raskolnikov was filled with disdain. His health was deteriorating. He suffered from fevers, chills, constant trembling, as well as from fitful sleep. He was no longer attending the university; he had put his career aside.

His solitary claim to status was an article he had written. In it he cleverly argued a kind of superman ethical theory, an idea inspired by Napoleon. The essence of the theory was the right of certain men to transgress the law. Raskolnikov gave different meanings to the theory. At times, this theory expressed for him a limitless individualism, an absolute defiance of the conventions of society. At other times, it voiced the more academic Hegelian notion that heroes give history its meaning. Their actions, whatever they be, transcend existing laws and moralities. Yet at other times, Raskolnikov professed by it a commitment to a redemptive socialism whose right to transgress the law and morality was to be found in the service of the downtrodden. Throughout the novel, Raskolnikov was caught up with this theory. It was a mask for the real spiritual game he was playing.[2]

At the outset of the novel the Raskolnikov whom we meet deliberates why he shouldn't kill the old, exploitative pawnbroker. She "is a stupid, senseless, insignificant, bad tempered, sick old hag, needed by no one and harmful to all. What does her life mean in the balance of existence? No more than the life of a louse or a cockroach. Not that much — because the old woman actually does harm. She eats up other people's lives."[3] Why not kill her, Raskolnikov asked, and "dedicate her money to serving mankind, to the general welfare?" "Hundreds, perhaps thousands of lives could be put on the right path, dozens of families rescued from poverty, from ruin, from collapse, from decay, from the venereal wards of the hospitals — all this with her money."[4] These thoughts remained for Raskolnikov more a matter of amusement for idle speculation than motives for action, until he received a letter from his mother.

His mother's letter brought home the overwhelming moral truth of his condition. He, who in theory was guilty of thinking all (*tous capable, tous coupable!*), became now, with the letter, guilty of sinning against those who loved him.

His mother's letter began: "You are all we have left, Dunia and I, you are everything, all our wishes and all our hope."[5] Each sentence added to his guilt. His mother said that she was stunned that he no longer was studying at the university and that he was no longer tutoring. She apologized for not having sent him money—but after all, she noted, her pension was set, and she had to pay back the money which she had borrowed for him in the past.

And then, with a single crushing blow, she explained what his sister Dunia had just suffered—and was yet to suffer on his account. For extra money Dunia had gone to work as a governess in the Svidrigailov household. Having taken a hundred rubles in advance on her salary, she was no longer in a position to quit when Mr. Svidrigailov first began to abuse her and then, no longer concealing his true passion, proposed to Dunia that she run off with him. His wife, Martha Petrovna, mistakenly blamed Dunia for the old man's infatuation and shamefully drove her out of the house. "Gossip that she was, she made Dunia and me a matter of public scandal for a whole month. Things went so far that Dunia and I could no longer go to Church. Fortunately Svidrigailov got hold of himself and repented, and Martha Petrovna not only came to us to beg our forgiveness, but then went about town reading a letter that entirely vindicated Dunia. Yet this doesn't solve the money problem, being Dunia can't return to work here," her mother added.

"Since then, however," Raskolnikov's mother continued, "Dunia has accepted an unexpected and pressing offer of marriage to a court councillor, Peter Petrovich Luzhin—a distant relative of Martha Petrovna, who came to know of our situation." Although the mother acknowledged that he is too abrupt, haughty, perhaps a bit morose, and altogether too blatant about his desire to marry a girl without dowry, still there could be no question about the husband being the benefactor of the wife.

Raskolnikov's mother, nevertheless, strove to praise Luzhin, at least to make him palatable to Raskolnikov: "He is a man of affairs, and busy. . . . He is a promising and prosperous man, has two official jobs, and already had money of his own. True, he is forty-five, but rather good looking and still attractive to women." The letter continues in this vein of rationalizing what is degrading. The mother even humiliatingly speculates on ways that this marriage of convenience might further Raskolnikov's career. Perhaps it might even produce a business partnership between him and Luzhin, she suggests.

The mother concludes her letter by mentioning that they will soon send Raskolnikov some money. She and Dunia will save a part of the money Luzhin gives them by economizing in their travel to Petersburg for the wedding. She expresses her hope that Raskolnikov would continue to pray, although she suspects that he has succumbed to the fad of unbelief. She ends her letter by making the most impossible request of all:

> Love your sister Dunia, Rodia. Love her as she loves you; and know that she loves you infinitely more than she loves herself. She is an angel; but you, Rodia, you are all we have—all our desire and all our hope. *If only you are happy, we will be happy.*[6]

What an impossible gift![7] What a moral burden to put on Raskolnikov! Even if his mother's letter had been written out of malice instead of love, the effects could not have been more devastating.[8] "When he finished reading, his face was pale and distorted by a twitch. A heavy bilious, angry smile played around his lips. . . . He thought for a long time. His heart beat powerfully, and powerfully his thoughts tumbled upon each other."[9] He, an only son, in a fatherless family—who for the last three years had lived parasitically off his mother and sister—had caused their reputation to be scandalized, driven his sister toward legal prostitution, and reduced his mother to such a state of desperation that "she consented to sacrifice a daughter for a son." Raskolnikov was now certain of only one thing: "As long as I'm alive this marriage will not take place; Mr. Luzhin can go to hell."[10] Never would he allow his sister to be purchased by a self-assured bourgeois, the worst possible type of person.[11]

Within a week his mother and sister, whom he had not seen for three years, were due to arrive to begin the arrangements for the wedding. Raskolnikov would greet them utterly empty-handed, unless he did something. Yet he had nothing to shield himself against their love and pity—nothing to show return for what they had given him in the past and what they now intended to sacrifice for him. He had to do something, anything! Only an action would express his defiance—serve somehow to separate himself from this totally degrading situation, of which he was the cause. Not to act, Raskolnikov said, was to "renounce life altogether. . . . Humbly accept my fate as it is, once and for all, strangle everything I have within me, and give up every right I have to act, to live, and to love."[12] Their humble love threatened him, a proud superman, with moral annihilation.

Delirious, frenzied, he took to the streets of Petersburg, hoping that unexpected occurrences, chance encounters, some sort of unexpected happening might save him. But he was only reminded of his situation by the poverty and the prostitution he saw on the streets. His obsession with the murder of the pawnbroker grew. In his fantasy the pawnbroker became himself and his mother. She was the culmination of all that is wrong. She was his despair, his hope. She was the only way out. Even one last prophetic dream, as if it were a gift sent from God to rescue him, could not deflect him from his murderous path.[13]

He dreamt of himself as a boy. In his dream, he sees a drunken peasant mercilessly whipping and beating an old nag of a horse. It pulls as hard as it can, yet it cannot move the cart. Increasing his beating and cursing, the peasant cruelly loads more and more people onto the cart. Finally the peasant kills the old nag, breaking its skull with a crow bar. Raskolnikov awoke from his dream shuddering. He resolved himself: He will not kill. He will not add his weight to those on the cart. His resolution, however, didn't hold. He was no longer in control of himself.

A few days later, as if he were possessed by an alien spirit, Raskolnikov set out to murder "the old nag. . . . As though someone were leading him by the hand and dragging him along irresistibly, blindly, with unnatural force, without objections. Just as though he had fallen like a piece of cloth into the wheel of a machine and it was beginning to draw him into the apparatus."[14] Everything took place unexpectedly and by chance. He took the ax not from the kitchen, as planned, but the porter's lodge. He killed not only the pawnbroker but her innocent saintly sister, Lizaveta. He had no idea how to commit robbery. He left the larger source of money untouched and didn't open the sack he did take. It was anything but a perfect crime. It was as though he were in a delirium. He forgot himself. He was not asleep, but in a state of oblivion.

He remained delirious for several days after the crime. He had fulfilled his wish. He would no longer have to bear the coming of his mother and sister. By murdering the pawnbroker, Raskolnikov had separated himself from them, as well as the moral community of the innocent. Raskolnikov (the root of whose name means division and suggests schism in Russian) had joined himself to those who persecute the innocent. What greater evil is there than to cause innocent suffering?

This is the basis of Raskolnikov's kinship with Marmeladov, the drunkard and ex-official. They met in a bar. Marmeladov had destroyed his family, not by pride, but by shameful drunkenness. In contrast to Raskolnikov, Marmeladov was not a character of guilt, but of shame. He could not stop drinking, hating himself, and talking. He made public the most secret sources of his shame. Openly he called himself "a pig . . . a beast by nature." He confessed to stealing the family's money, "even drinking up his wife's stocking money." His wife was dying of consumption. In his pitiful, tortured mind, drinking had become not only his way of life but a search for salvation. "That is why I drink, I look for compassion. I look for feeling — I drink because I want to suffer."[15] Yet he claims that he wants no compassion, no pity: "I need to be crucified, not pitied! Crucified!" Worst of all, his sins were driving his oldest daughter, Sonia, to prostitution. She must sell herself so that his wife and children, from whom he stole, can survive. Sonia was the victim of his sins. Marmeladov continued to believe in mercy. Christ will not only save her, but him too, Marmeladov believes, for her sacrifice is so great. Christ will forgive even him — shameless coward and sinner that he is!

Marmeladov died in Sonia's arms, begging her forgiveness. Showing that the sources of the good were not entirely depleted within him, Raskolnikov took pity on Marmeladov's family. He gave the widow Katerine Ivanova, all his money for Marmeladov's burial and the wake. That wake turned into a humiliating scandal.[16] There, in the presence of the least pleasant, uninvited, and drunken company, Katerine Ivanova and her German landlady exchanged the bitterest insults. The detestable Luzhin, Raskolnikov's sister's fiancée, tried unsuccessfully to blame Sonia for stealing from him, so as to turn sister and mother against Raskolnikov. The wake ended in a raucous brawl. The landlady, hit by a glass, began to throw the Marmeladov household goods about; Katerine Ivanova, half dead with coughing, feebly attacked the landlady, who easily cast her aside and called for her family's eviction.

After the wake Raskolnikov again went to Sonia. At stake in Raskolnikov's meeting with Sonia was the question whether he would repent and atone or succumb to evil and self-hate.[17] Dostoevsky described the latter alternative in terms of the character Svidrigailov, Raskolnikov's spider-like dark double. Svidrigailov murdered his wife and her servant, then corrupted and thus caused the suicide of a young girl.[18] He then killed himself. By going to Sonia, Raskolnikov had already taken a precarious and hesitant step away from the evil that consumed Svidrigailov. He was admitting, perhaps only on some deep subconscious level, that this gentle, self-sacrificing creature had something he needed. Perhaps he could give her something she needed. The possibility of this exchange offered Raskolnikov the hope that he could renew his relations with humanity.

Against Sonia's faith, Raskolnikov tried his worst venom. He attacked her suffering itself: "How skinny you are! Look at your hand! Transparent. Fingers like a corpse's." He shamed her for prostitution. He asked whether her mother used to beat her. He told her that her mother was terribly ill, incurably insane, and soon to die. He asked how she alone would be able to care for the children and, more perversely, suggested that her younger sister, Polia, would end up as Sonia had, an impoverished prostitute. And as if that were not enough, Raskolnikov, with inquisitorial probing, attacked her refuge: "Maybe there's no God at all." He told the sobbing Sonia, "You say your mother's mind is going. Your mind is going."

Yet at the end of this brutal attack, peering into her grief-filled face, his lips trembling, "suddenly and swiftly he bowed down, fell to the floor and kissed her foot. . . . Sonia drew back from him in horror, as from a madman. 'What are you doing that for, to me of all people?!' she muttered and turned pale. He rose at once. 'It wasn't you I bowed down to. I bowed down to all of suffering humanity.'"[19]

No sooner had he shown this compassion, than he launched another venomous attack against her. He attacked the very value of her sacrifice, which was her reason for staying alive: "All you have to do is open your eyes—you won't help anybody this way, you won't save anybody from anything! . . . Tell me, then finally [he was almost in a frenzy] how can you abide such shame and degradation inside you up against their opposite—such holy feelings? Wouldn't it have been better, a thousand times more 'right'—and more clever too—if you'd gone and jumped in the river and ended everything at once!"[20]

Deeply wounded by the assault, Sonia was bewildered and terrified. She could only reply: "If she were no more who would care for her mother and the children." And she asked: "What would I be without God . . . He does everything!" In the face of her faith, Raskolnikov concluded, "She's a holy fool, a holy fool."[21] This idea grew on him as he listened to her while she read from the Bible the story of Lazarus, as he commanded. Sonia, the holy fool, he thought, transgresses the law just as he had, but not by an act of selfish will, but out of selfless love. She was living beyond the law for the sake of others. He had transgressed the law to escape others.

Raskolnikov found the possibility of community with Sonia. "I have abandoned my family. . . . You are all I have now. We are both damned so let's go together." She didn't understand him. "She only knew that he was terribly, infinitely unhappy."[22]

Raskolnikov left Sonia, promising that if he were to return, he would tell her who killed her good friend, Lizaveta. (Sonia and

Lizaveta, both holy fools, had consecrated their friendship by the exchange of crosses.) To return to Sonia was agony. It was to confess. It was to abandon his independence. It was to cause another person to suffer on his behalf.

Yet if he were to return to the community of the good, he had to confess. Confession was his only remaining gift. He would have humiliatingly to give up his secret, the refuge of his pride. Yet this was the only way back to the community of the innocent, the community of the suffering and the good![23]

Raskolnilov did return to Sonia, confessing that he killed the pawnbroker and her sister, Sonia's friend, Lizaveta.[24] Sonia embraced him. She asked why he had taken it upon himself to commit this horrid deed. "There is nobody anywhere in the world," she said, "unhappier than you!"[25] And to Raskolnikov's question, "whether she would leave him," she replied: "No, no never, nowhere! . . . I follow you, I'll go anywhere."

Sonia's display of love only compounded Raskolnikov's guilt. Again he was being loved; accepted as he would not accept himself. Raskolnikov retreated from this humbling, though overwhelming love: the gift for which he again found himself with nothing to return. This time he turned against himself, not Sonia. "Because on my own I couldn't bear it, and came to dump my burden on somebody else: If you suffer, too, I'll find it easier! Can you love that kind of scoundrel?" He tore at himself, unveiling layer after layer of his own confusion of why he killed: "to be Napoleon. . . . No! . . . To start a new career. . . . No! . . . Sonia, I only killed a louse—useless, vile, pernicious. . . . I got angry, really angry at my condition, and I hid myself in the corner of my room like a spider. . . wanted to try. . . . I simply killed; I killed for myself alone. . . . Whether I'd become anybody's benefactor or spend my whole life like a spider catching everybody in my web and sucking the living juices out of them—at that moment it should have been all the same to me!"[26]

To these twisting, tormenting, self-accusations, Sonia replied in the only language she knew: "You abandoned God, and God has stricken you, and turned you over to the Devil!"[27] And then, after asserting that it was not the old hag he killed, but "myself forever! But it was the Devil who killed the old hag—not me! . . . Enough, Sonia, Enough! Let me be!" Faced with the torment of this self-exorcism, Sonia cried out in anguish "How you are suffering!" And in face of this Raskolnikov admitted for the first time this utter helplessness. His face monstrously distorted with despair, he asked: "Well tell me what should I do now!"[28] And as if she were no longer the innocent-child prostitute of Petersburg but the Virgin of Heaven, Sonia instructed Raskolnikov with the highest wisdom and authority:

> Go now. Go this very moment, and stand at the crossroads; bow down, and first kiss the earth which you have defiled; then bow down to the whole world, to the four points of the compass, and say aloud, for all men to hear: 'I have killed!' Then God will send you life again.[29]

Does this mean "I am to give myself up? Go to Siberia?" Raskolnikov asked. "Yes," Sonia replied. And as though she were voicing Dostoevsky's final wisdom, Sonia instructed Raskolnikov: "You must accept suffering and redeem yourself by it." Raskolnikov insisted that he wouldn't go; he was still a man, he would put up a fight.

Her love weighed heavy upon him. It had breached the walls of pride that had enclosed his heart. There was no doubt that he would return to Sonia, take the cross of Lizaveta which Sonia had offered him, kiss the crossroads, and there confess to the world and ask for forgiveness. His regeneration was underway.

Dostoevsky did not quickly kill off the demons which inhabited Raskolnikov's spirit. Raskolnikov continued to try to live by his proud thought. He persisted in rationalizing his crime. He kept playing cat and mouse with the patient, clever police inspector, Porfiry Petrovitch. He continued to rebel against the stupid baseness of his crime. Above all else, he repeatedly suffered the shameful recognition that he had killed Lizaveta, another Holy Fool like Sonia. . . . "Poor creatures meek!" He could not have shed more innocent blood. He had murdered innocence, sacrificed it so that he could escape his sister's choice to sacrifice herself for him.

Raskolnikov's murder had succeeded in stopping him from having to accept his sister's sacrifice. Yet the cost of his violent crime of will was a pact with the Devil. He had joined those who cause suffering, instead of those, like Sonia, who bear suffering.

On the eve of his confession, Raskolnikov bade his mother and sister farewell. Raskolnikov threw himself at his mother's feet, and she—her mind increasingly failing—gave him her blessing. They embraced and wept together; their tears joined them, as words could not. The mother never knew of her son's crime; she had lost her mind. No doubt, that was the price she paid to avoid being conscious of her son's awful crime. Dunia, who knew of her brother's crime, forgave him, and told him: "By going to suffer, surely you wash away half of your crime."[30]

After picking up the cross at Sonia's, Raskolnikov began his "sorrowful way," *via dolorosa*.[31] Sonia followed behind. Along the streets, he gave out a five kopeck piece to a beggar. At the crossroads, as if he were obeying deeper forces within himself, he melted inside, threw himself down and kissed the earth. (A nearby youth remarked: "He's plastered!")

Glancing behind, he caught sight of Sonia. "At this moment, Raskolnikov understood *once and for all*, that Sonia would be with him always. She would follow him to the ends of the earth, wherever fate might send him. His heart heaved. . . . But now he had come to the fated place."[32] At his request she had made herself a gift to him. She was his. And now, at work within him were forces of love. He had found a love he could accept, and that love would ransom his heart, purchase his restoration.

Raskolnikov's "crime and punishment" had, in contradiction to all rational ethics, nothing to do with the civil law, and everything to do with the laws of the human heart and God.[33]

There was one last cycle in the struggle between an isolating pride and a redeeming love. During his first year in Siberia, Raskolnikov experienced resentment that fate had dealt him such a blow, shame that he had acted so stupidly, anger that he had not killed himself, and bitterness that he was not more remorseful. All the while Sonia patiently ministered to him. One warm day, Raskolnikov was working at the river side. As if by magic, Sonia, whom he had begun truly to need, appeared at his side. His being was transfused with love. As she read his eyes, "there was no longer any doubt he loved her. He loved her infinitely. . . . Tears came. Love resurrected them; the heart of one contained the infinite sources of life for the heart of the other."[34]

Like Lazarus, he was resurrected. He could love again, he could give good for good. Henceforth, he could stand as an equal in her sight. He had joined the community of man.

ELEMENTAL EXCHANGES

Dostoevsky's vision of the redeeming gift of suffering had many sources. It was rooted in his personal life. Literary and financial quarrels with fellow writers and editors supplied him with intimate knowledge of scandal, envy, pettiness, and resentment. Living on the edge of scarcity and hungering for recognition, Dostoevsky's life had a desperate frenzy about it. He had to scheme to survive. And because he did, there is little wonder that Dostoevsky divided the world into extremes. His characters are either the well-to-do or the poor, victims or victimizers. For Dostoevsky life was frost or furnace.[35]

Dostoevsky's intimate relations were marked by great ambivalence. He had the darkest, most divided feelings about his father, whom he believed was killed by his own peasants. He wrestled with his feelings about his mother. She was for him both the object of great thankfulness for how much she had given him and of great resentment for how much she expected from him.

Dostoevsky also felt a crucial sense of an unpayable debt to his sister and his wife. The model of Raskolnikov's sister was Dostoevsky's own sister, whose marriage was to the advantage of Dostoevsky and his older brother, Michael. Also Dostoevsky experienced an overwhelming sense of indebtedness to his young wife, Anna, who for the last fifteen years of his life was his Sonia. She bore his children, prepared his manuscripts, and stood firm when he suffered the grief of a child's death, raged over a rejected manuscript, and alternately was taken by feverish fits of gambling and long bouts of remorse.[36]

Dostoevsky also resented Anna's love. Her love made him feel like he was a child, a sinner, and a parasite. This resentment not only showed in his characters like Raskolnikov, but it was also expressed in his fiction by his attraction for the *femme fatale*.

Other personal experiences confirmed Dostoevsky's belief that only the loving embrace of the mother gave life worth. He stood helplessly by when his children died. He knew life was filled with pain and suffering which could not be escaped; injustices which could not be rectified, situations against which human will was impotent. As a young man, he had stood before the Tsar's sham firing squad. As a mature man, he was under the sentence of increasing epileptic seizures which made death seem terrifyingly near, ever unpredictably present. The comfort of a woman's love was, in Dostoevsky's view, solace for human limits.

Other elements explain Dostoevsky's identification of the good with woman's love and innocent suffering. Dostoevsky was a romantic. He was susceptible to themes of the struggles of the proud and the demonic, as well as quests for happiness, community, and innocence. He was also a Russian intellectual, which meant everything was exaggerated. They, the culture carriers of the nation, had before them the constant choice of whether or not the Russian people should imitate Western ways.[37]

Under the reactionary regime of Nicholas I (1825–1855), to be an intellectual, as the young Dostoevsky discovered, was a dangerous profession. To suggest that Russia, like Europe, should have a constitution, free its serfs, and allow a free press could mean prison, exile, death. Herzen said: "It is a strange thing that almost all our day-dreams ended in Siberia or the scaffold and hardly ever in triumph."[38]

In his youth, Dostoevsky embraced the secular progressive philosophy of the West. In his mature years, upon his return from Siberia, he rejected progressive European ideals, in favor of Russian nationalism and Orthodox Christianity.

Europe became for Dostoevsky a matter of passionate negation; Russia, an object of religious faith.[39] Europe stood for pride, willfulness, materialism, individualism, calculating pragmatism, the exploiting bourgeois; Russia for humility, suffering, giving. Europe's Roman Catholic Church and socialism were, for Dostoevsky, power-hungry. He even went so far as to assert that even Europe's workers had become "capitalists, par excellence." In Dostoevsky's vision, Europe was dead. It had lost the meaning of brotherhood and the principle of the sacrifice.

Contrariwise, Russsia, for Dostoevsky, had a holy mission; it was a God-bearing nation. Russia, Dostoevsky argued, was saved by its social and economic "backwardness." Socially organized around the communal village (mir), the Russian peasant was still free of the West's selfish individualism. In the heart of the Russian peasant there was still a pure image of Christ and of Mary.

> And their ideals are vigorous and sacred; they have saved the people during the ages of their martyrdom. These ideals have grown into their very soul, rewarding it with candor and honesty, with sincerity and a broad, all-receptive mind—and all these, in an attractive, harmonious blending. If, despite this, there is so much filth, the Russian himself suffers from it most and believes that it is something alluvial and transient, a diabolical suggestion; that darkness will disappear and perpetual light will beam.[40]

In Dostoevsky's vision, Russia stood for the spiritual. Russia was a community formed by a love of God, instead of by the laws and the interests of men. Russia, free of European egoism, had for its mission the service of humanity. "Russia," Dostoevsky declared, "in conjunction with Slavdom, will utter to the whole world the greatest word ever heard, and that word will precisely be a covenant of universal human fellowship."[41]

Beyond the vulgar nationalism of Dostoevsky's view, his vision was uniquely personal.[42] He idealized Russia to be the home he desperately hungered for. He mythologized Russia to be a suffering people, a new Israel, the victim-savior of mankind; all those things he felt about himself. Russia was, for Dostoevsky, all the pain he suffered and all the earthly and heavenly happiness for which he hoped.

Dostoevsky's view of Russia reveals the essence of his ethical philosophy. In diametrical opposition to the egoists who define the good in relation to the individual and the utilitarians who define it in reference to the good of the majority, Dostoevsky conceived the good as inseparable from man's relation to God.

In Dostoevsky's view, man is not the lord of his own spirit. He cannot will his own peace, he cannot define his own good.

The good, for Dostoevsky, is a *gift of God*. Though he did not argue for the theological doctrines of predestination or justification by faith alone, he argued against the saving power of human knowledge and will. Dostoevsky always conceived man to be struggling against a damning pride.

For Dostoevsky the good is from God. Creation, Providence, and Grace—for these divine gifts man can only be thankful. Man's thankfulness must be expressed by imitation of Christ, Mary, and the saints. According to Dostoevsky, man must make his life a perpetual sacrifice to God. Man owes himself as a gift to God.

Like the most ancient teachers, Dostoevsky preached gratitude, reverential piety, as the first step to the good. He made the heart the first source of our ethics. Ethics, above all else, is tied to religion. This was an ancient vision. And just how ancient we modern individuals are is revealed by how much we are moved by Dostoevsky's apocalyptic tales of great pride confronted by suffering innocence.

NOTES

1. For general introductions to Dostoevsky, see Konstantin Mochulsky's *Dostoevsky, His Life and Work,* trans. Michael Minihan (Princeton, 1967) and Avrahm Yarmolinsky's *Dostoevsky, Work and Days* (New York, 1971); for Dostoevsky's youth, of use is Joseph Frank's *Dostoevsky, The Seeds of Revolt, 1821-1849* (Princeton, 1976). For his tie to the literature of period, see Donald Fanger's *Dostoevsky and Romantic Realism. A Study of Dostoevsky in Relation to Balzac, Dickens, and Gogol* (Chicago, 1965). For useful introductions to ideas and movements of the era, see J. L. Talmon's *Romanticism and Revolt, Europe 1815-1848* (New York, 1967), Charles Morazé's *The Triumph of the Middle Classes* (New York, 1968), Benedetto Croce's *History of Europe in the Nineteenth Century* (New York, 1963), and E. J. Hobsbawm's *Age of Revolution, 1789-1848* (New York, 1962), 323.

2. In his "Afterword" to *Crime and Punishment* (New York, 1968), Sidney

Monas sees Dostoevsky's conception of Raskolnikov as superman influenced by Bazarov, nihilist hero of Turgenev's *Fathers and Sons*, iron willed Rakhmetov of Chernyshevsky's *What Is To Be Done?*, Rastignac of Balzac's *Le père Goriot*, Hermann of Pushkin's *Queen of Spades*, and Julien Sorel of Stendhal's *Red and Black*. It is this translation of *Crime and Punishment* which is cited here, unless otherwise indicated.

3. *Ibid.*, 73.
4. *Ibid.*
5. Letter is found *Ibid.*, 40-47.
6. *Ibid.*, 40. Emphasis is mine.
7. Near the end of my research I discovered that in his "The Counterpoint of Experience," *Crime and Punishment*, ed. George Gibran (New York, 1975), 621-622, R. D. Laing also stressed the devastating psychological assault that mother's letter makes upon Raskolnikov. In Laing's language it constitutes "a non-compossible set of positions all at once; it contains an implicit injunction to collude at each of the multi-levels of hypocrisy, including having a religious belief that is dead; it demands a happiness which it, the letter, makes shameful to have; it makes his sister an angel before whom he must bow, yet if he were really a man, he would defend; he is told to suppress all his feelings about the situation and Mr. Luzhin, yet to do so in the name of a love that would not endorse the evil plan underway.
8. In early drafts of *Crime and Punishment*, as found in the *Notebooks for Crime and Punishment*, ed. and trans. Edward Wasiolek (Chicago, 1967), the antagonistic relation between Raskolnikov and his mother was not repressed. She gets angry at Raskolnikov and demands total obedience from him, while Raskolnikov for his part, finds her caresses a burden. In the final draft, Dostoevsky purified not only Raskolnikov's love for his mother, but his love for Sonia and Dunia. However, as I suggest in this essay, Dostoevsky constantly was at war with the overwhelming power of the self-sacrificing love of women, be it in the form of mother, sister, or lover. This theme in all its ambivalent depths makes it, in my opinion, more important for understanding Dostoevsky than the classical Freudian struggle between son and father. Of course, also to be borne in mind is the all pervasive power of a romanticism whose preoccupation with women was characterized by the extremes of woman either as innocent saint or corrupting temptress.
9. *Crime and Punishment*, 40.
10. *Ibid.*, 48.
11. The hate of the bourgeoisie, on the one hand, and identity with the outcast, on the other, had already become by the 1830s a common characteristic of the Western intellectual *avant-garde* Theda Shapiro, *Painters and Politics, The European Avant-Garde and Society, 1900-1925* (New York, 1976), 9-11.
12. *Crime and Punishment*, 53.
13. Dream is found, *ibid.*, 62-67.
14. *Ibid.*, 302.
15. *Ibid.*, 303.
16. This scene of public scandal, described *ibid.*, 370-394, reminds one of

Dostoevsky's "A Nasty Story." A "superior" bureaucrat, "as an act of charity," invites himself to an employee's wedding. There he gets disgustingly drunk, vomits in the wedding bed where he has been put to sleep. This so disgusts the bride she refuses the marriage with the employee. However, the bureaucrat is "good enough" not to fire the employee for having behaved so embarrassingly in front of him," *Gambler, Bobok, A Nasty Story*, (Middlesex, England, 1966), 185-238.

17. Their first encounter is found, *Crime and Punishment*, 308-323.

18. In his wanton, self-destructive pursuit of pleasure, his violation of the young girl (a sin with which Dostoevsky was preoccupied) and his suicide, Svidrigailov clearly anticipates Rogozhim of *The Idiot* and Stavrogin of *The Possessed*.

19. *Ibid.*, 315.

20. *Ibid.*

21. *Ibid.*, 317.

22. *Ibid.*, 321.

23. The exchange of secrets and intimacies is among the most common and yet most subtle way for people to join themselves to one another. Dostoevsky knew much about this sort of human commerce.

24. Their second encounter is found *Ibid.*, 394-409.

25. *Ibid.*, 400.

26. *Ibid.*, 402-406.

27. *Ibid.*, 406.

28. *Ibid.*, 407.

29. *Ibid.*

30. *Ibid.*, 498-499.

31. Their third encounter is found *Ibid.*, 501-504.

32. *Ibid.*, 506. Emphasis is mine.

33. In *House of the Dead* (1862) Dostoevsky remarks at several points on how "the crime and punishment" of those he knew in Siberia didn't at all correspond with their evil character.

34. *Ibid.*, 527.

35. From his earliest work *The Poor Folk* (1846), through *The Insulted and the Injured* (1861) to *The Brothers* (1880), Dostoevsky divided the world into the oppressed and the oppressors. Fanger says that it is this division between victim and victimizer that gives Dostoevsky's essentially "psychological tales the character of a social drama," *Dostoevsky and Romantic Realism*, 57.

36. Aside from the works of Frank, Mochulsky, and Yarmolinsky, for Dostoevsky's relation to women, see Anna Dostoevsky's *Dostoevsky, Reminiscences*, trans. Beatrice Stillman (New York, 1975).

37. Marc Raeff, *The Eighteenth Century Nobility* (New York, 1966), 80.

38. Alexander Herzen, *My Past and Thought*, trans. Constance Garnett (New York, 1973), 65.

39. To move in extremes was a characteristic of the Russian intelligentsia, esp. of the first generation; the lives and thoughts of Bakunin, Herzen, and

Belinsky amply testify to this. The latter—whose praise of Dostoevsky's *The Poor Folk* gave Dostoevsky a reputation—said of Dostoevsky's nature: "It always runs to extremes." He said of his early conversion to socialism: "The idea of socialism has become for me the idea of ideas, the essence of being, the question of questions, the Alpha and Omega of Faith and Knowledge," Hare, 54. Dostoevsky's later brutal attack against the West in general, and France and its people in particular, is found in Dostoevsky's *Summer Impressions*, trans. Kyril Fitzlyon (London, 1955), 70-94.

40. Feodor Dostoevsky, *Diary of the Writer*, Vol. I (New York, 1973), 202-203. For a discussion of the notion of holy Russia, harkening back to the millennarian theme of Russia as "The Third Rome," see V. V. Zenkovskii, *Russian Thinkers and Europe*, trans. Galia Bodde (Ann Arbor, 1953), esp. 154-170.

41. *Diary of the Writer*, Vol. II, 578.

42. For initiating a critical discussion of Dostoevsky's political views, see Irving Howe's *Politics and the Novel* (New York, 1957), 51-75; Hans Kohn *Pan-Slavism*, (New York, 1960), 208-217, and his *Prophets and Peoples* (New York, 1961), 122-146. More sympathetic treatments are found in Nicholas Berdyaev's *Dostoevsky*, trans. Donald Attwater (New York, 1974) and Nicholas Zernov, *The Russian Religious Renaissance* (London, 1963).

CHAPTER FOUR

Friedrich Nietzsche: Beyond Good and Evil

WHAT IS THE PLACE of the self in the realm of values? What gives the self its value? Does the self's importance lie in its uniqueness or its universality? Is the self of worth because of what God or society gives it?

One line of inquiry about the worth of the self can be suggested by the following questions: Is the individual will the essential element of morality? Is good the result of actions by the strong individual?

Friedrich Nietzsche (1844–1900) answered these two questions in the affirmative. It was as though he were the living philosophical embodiment of Dostoevsky's Raskolnikov. His ethical theory called for a superman who would negate all the values of the West and revalue existence itself. Nietzsche was the most violent philosopher of the individual in modern history.[1]

Nietzsche's intellectual life was a constant, and often pathetic, struggle to remain forever as no human can: free of all association, absolutely protean in possibilities. His struggle for autonomy put him on a collision course with his age whose dominating forces were new collectivities. His age, the predecessor of our own, was caught up in the business of building national societies, and struggling for control of the newly emerging urban industrial order.[2] During the last half of the nineteenth century, approximately 85 percent of the entire population of Europe was on the move. Peasants were being lured and shoved, with varying degrees of success, into becoming national citizens. The public school, social welfare, suffrage, the military draft, went hand in hand with expanding highways, railroads, and economic markets. The old was being transformed into the new. There were wars of selfish interests and enlightened ideals attempting to undo centuries of old traditions, while at the same time create new loyalties.

Nietzsche's reaction to his age was extreme. His indictments of the bourgeois were especially shrill, particularly in dealing with the pretentiousness of the bourgeois *nouveaux riches*. He brutally attacked the conformist instincts of the socialists; the sickly pieties and the debilitating altruisms of the do-gooders; the literary niceties of the tender-hearted, decadent romantics. Nietzsche made it his duty to seek out and destroy "the new barbarism . . . the new animal-herd morality" that afflicted Europe with the idea that "one now knew what Socrates thought he did not know: what is good and evil."[3]

Nietzsche's critiques read as an index of what he took to be the prevailing errors of his time:

> Critique of modern man (his moralistic mendaciousness): – the "good man" corrupted and seduced by bad institutions (tyrants and priests); – reason as authority; – history as overcoming of errors; – the future as progress; – the Christian state ("the Lord of hosts") – the Christian sex impulse (or marriage); – the kingdom of "justice" (the cult of "humanity"); – "freedom."
>
> The romantic pose of modern man: – the noble man (Byron, Victor Hugo, George Sand); – noble indignation; – consecration through passion (as true "nature"); – siding with the oppressed and underprivileged: motto of the historians and novelists; – the Stoics of duty; – selflessness as art and knowledge; – altruism as the most mendacious form of egoism (utilitarianism), most sentimental egoism.[4]

Throughout his writings Nietzsche gave different, and often irreconcilable, appraisals of the meaning of life. At points he voiced views based upon the starkest Darwinism: life is only a struggle of the strongest for survival. At other points, he postulated "the will to power," a mysterious vital force. And at other points, he idealized life as a creation of heroic deeds. Nietzsche always judged that which served life to be good, and that which impeded it, bad. This was the premise of his first major work, *The Birth of Tragedy* (1872).

There he defined the essence of Greek tragedy as "an Appollonian embodiment of Dionysiac insights and powers."[5] For Nietzsche the successful tragedian, like Aeschylus or Sophocles, must bring together the vitality of Dionysiac life forces (the primitive, the sexual, the will) with the Appollonian spirit of the rational (the image, the dream, the ideal). The betrayal of tragedy and life – which Nietzsche judged to be the sin of his own age – occurred when tension between the Dionysian and the Appollonian was broken. Nietzsche considered tragedy to be betrayed when either irrational forces triumphed over man (as they did in Eurpides' plays) or when human reason exercised a corrosive influence upon instinctual life.

Defying all idealizations of Greek rationality, the young Nietzsche argued, "Wisdom is a crime against nature";[6] "Socrates' great Cyclop's eye – that eye which never glowed with the artist's divine frenzy – turned upon tragedy."[7] Socrates and his followers did something worse than to claim to make the world knowable. They claimed it was teachable. "[They] considered all noble deeds, compassion, self-sacrifice, heroism, even that spiritual calm . . . to be ultimately derived from the dialectic of knowledge."[8]

For Nietzsche tragedy must be vital. To be vital it must be both destructive and creative. In fact, in the young Nietzsche's romantic eyes, creation requires destruction. Tragedy is to destroy the myths, the ideals, and the culture that restrain life, and hence, to incite the individual to create a new meaning for life. Tragedy, according to Nietzsche, liberates man to make himself a work of art.[9] In Nietzsche's tragic vision, man must perpetually struggle for meaning, for man is only what he creates himself to be, yet all that he creates is mortal. Man must create, in great agony, yet his creations are never permanent. Life demands art be destroyed. So, in the eternal cycle of Nietzsche's view, art destroys and is destroyed.

For Nietzsche, tragedy and destruction pervade all nature and history.[10] We know this and must accept it. The hero, Nietzsche said, "the highest manifestation of the will, is destroyed, and we assent, since he too is merely a phenomenon, and the eternal life of the will remains unaffected."[11] Life calls for art and life destroys art. "There are on the one hand the spirit of the *sublime* which subjugates terror by means of art; on the other hand the *comic* spirit, which releases us, through art, from the tedium of absurdity."[12]

This aesthetic consciousness separated Nietzsche from his age. It gave him a sense of superiority, a sense of being on "a mountain peak of lonely contemplation where he will have few companions."[13] He called his age spiritless: "Every culture that has lost myth has lost, by the same token, its natural creativity. . . . Only a horizon ringed about the myths can unify a culture."[14] He judged his age to be abstract, to be without myth, thus devoid of culture; an age of abstract law, and abstract government; "a culture without any fixed and consecrated place of origin, condemned to exhaust possibilities and feed miserably and parasitically on every culture under the sun. . . . Here we have our present age, the result of a Socratism bent on extermination of myth."[15] Nietzsche prophesied: "Socratic man has run his course."[16]

"All that is now called culture, education, civilization, will one day have to appear before the incorruptible judge, Dionysus."[17]

This theme was to be a constant part of his writings thereafter. In his description of the *Genealogy of Morals*, offered in *Ecce Homo*, Nietzsche wrote:

> That new party of life which would tackle the greatest of all tasks, the attempt to raise humanity higher, including the relentless destruction of everything that was degenerating and parasitical, would again make possible that excess of life on earth from which the Dionysian state, too, would have to awaken again. I promise a tragic age: the highest art in saying Yes to life, tragedy, will be reborn when humanity has weathered the consciousness of the hardest but most necessary wars without suffering from it.[18]

This tragic aesthetic consciousness inspired Nietzsche's thoughts on history. In *The Use and Abuse of History* (1873), Nietzsche directed history to the same therapeutic ends as he had tragedy. History should destroy what blocks life and foster what ignites the will.

"Historical study is only fruitful for the future," Nietzsche claimed, "if it follows a powerful life-giving influence."[19] An antiquarian history, which mindlessly accumulated the stuff of the past, could choke off the present. A monumental history, which celebrated the greatness of the past, casts the shadow of inferiority over the present. Monumental history can even be, Nietzsche wrote, "the cloak under which (the little men's) hatred of present power and greatness masquerades as an extreme admiration of the past."[20] "I hate everything," Nietzsche quoted Goethe to say in the first line of his *Use and Abuse of History* "that merely instructs me without increasing or directly quickening my activity."[21] Elsewhere Nietzsche described history "as an enormous heap of indigestible knowledge-stones."[22]

Nietzsche preached a critical history, a history which instructed that for life forgetting is as important as remembering. "Everything," Nietzsche remarked, "that is born is worthy of being destroyed."[23] Critical history, Nietzsche argued, should bring "the past to the bar of judgment, interrogate it remorselessly, and finally condemn it. Every past is worth condemning; this is the rule in mortal affairs, which always contain a large measure of human power and human weakness."[24] "One who cannot leave the past behind on the threshold of the moment and forget the past, who cannot stand on a single point like a goddess of victory, without fear or giddiness, will never know what happiness is, and, worse still, will never do anything to make others happy."[25]

Nietzsche's critical history was praise of Goethe's conscienceless man of action: "He . . . is without conscience, he is also without knowledge: he forgets most things in order to do one, he is unjust to what is behind him, and only recognizes one law – the law of that which is to be."[26] Already at this stage, Nietzsche can be understood to be supporting the myth of the superman – the man who will be the life force of a new order.

In the *Genealogy of Morals* (1887) Nietzsche aims directly at his age's conscience, the source of his era's anti-life impulses. In advance of Freud by a generation, Nietzsche understood that the nature of society itself results in repression:

> All instincts that are not allowed free play turn inward. This is what I call man's interiorization; it alone provides the soil for the growth of what is later called man's *soul*. Man's interior world, originally meager and tenuous, was expanding in every dimension in proportion as the outward discharge of feeling was curtailed. . . .[27]

To be a member of any society, Nietzsche argued, is to have inside oneself a set of ideals about the good, the true, and the beautiful which serve as an inner censure of all one's instincts. Civilization meant repression for Nietzsche. Contemporary civilization, in Nietzsche's opinion, had the most destructively repressive conscience.

In Nietzsche's view one source of that repressive-guilt morality was the growth of rational individualism. As if he were speaking in advance for a host of twentieth century thinkers, Nietzsche wrote in the *Gay Science* (1887) of the dread of being the solitary individual.

> During the longest and most remote periods of the human past, the sting of conscience was not at all what it is now. Today one feels responsible only for one's will and actions, and one finds one's pride in oneself. All our teachers of law start from this sense of self and pleasure in the individual, as if this had always been the fount of law. But during the longest period of the human past nothing was more terrible to feel than that one stood by oneself. To be alone, to experience things by oneself, neither to obey nor to rule, to be an individual – that was not a pleasure but a punishment; one was sentenced to individuality.[28]

Nietzsche considered "slave morality" as another source of the contemporary guilt. Slave morality came to birth in the resentful person, a creature who, too weak and fearful to compete with others, seeks by thought the nobility which he cannot have in action. The resentful man—that "diminished, hopelessly mediocre, and savorless contemporary type"—teaches weakness, "the ethics of pity."[29] Sympathy, empathy, charity, and equality—these were the composing elements of the ethics of pity. In Tolstoi's mindless love of all, in the socialist's infatuation with the downtrodden, in the reformers' cosmic altruism, Nietzsche found enemies of the vital and of the strong.

Slave morality was, according to Nietzsche, the result of a negative rebellion. Drawing on his training as a philologist, Nietzsche demonstrated that early languages identify the aristocratic with the good, the noble with the generous and the fine, and conversely, they associate the bad with the base, the common, the simple, the meager. The good was not a creation of repressive thought. Certainly it was not a matter of self-abnegation. But it was, Nietzsche concluded, a creation of the aristocrats who acted strongly, spontaneously, innocently. They did what they did because it was what life and station required. *Resentment was not theirs.*[30]

The slave, according to Nietzsche, was unlike the aristocrat, a creation of opposition. Noble life filled him with envy, jealousy, and resentment. Guilt, morality, and conscience were his favorite means to attack the noble. The slave only had for a life his dark broodings about it; he had nothing to affirm but his resentment. This was his value. "The slave revolt in morality," Nietzsche summarized his views, "begins when *ressentiment* itself becomes creative and gives birth to values: the *ressentiment* of natures that are denied the true reaction, that of deeds, and compensate themselves with an imaginary revenge."[31]

The priests—"the greatest haters in history"—are the ideologues of the slaves.[32] Bad conscience is their profession. "It is their impotence which makes their hate so violent and sinister, so cerebral and poisonous."[33]

Of all the groups who were responsible for the introduction of slave morality into the spirit of the West, the Jews were most responsible according to Nietzsche. He called them "the most priestly people of all." Nietzsche wrote, "Whatever else has been done to damage the powerful and the great of this earth seems trivial compared with what the Jews have done, that priestly people who succeeded in avenging themselves on their enemies and oppressors by radically inverting all their values, that is by an act of the most spiritual vengeance."[34] Nietzsche described their revolutionary *inversion of morals*:

> It was the Jew who, with frightening consistency, dared to invert the aristocratic value equations good/noble/powerful/beautiful/happy/

favored-of-the-gods and maintain, with the furious hatred of the underprivileged and impotent, that 'only the poor, the powerless, are good; only the suffering, sick, and ugly, truly blessed. But you noble and mighty ones of the earth will be, to all eternity, the evil, the cruel, the avaricious, the godless, and thus the cursed and damned!'[35]

In addition to slave morality and repression, Nietzsche postulated another source of the guilty conscience. Taking his cue from the German word *Schuld* (which has its root in the verb *Schulden* which means to be indebted), Nietzsche argued that all archaic and primitive peoples conceived their transactions as involving a creditor and a debtor. Nietzsche saw the debtor's conscience formed around a recognition of what he had been given and what he must give in return. The debtor's state of being beholden was recognized not only by the creditor's right to find his remuneration among the debtor's good (including wife and children) but his additional right to have his compensation by "exercising his cruelty on another." One purpose of punishment, Nietzsche wrote, "consists of the payments of damages to the injured party."[36] Nietzsche sought to find the creditor's compensation in punishment in that well known German concept, *Schadenfreude*: one gains pleasure in another's suffering. It is especially pleasurable to cause that suffering since it testifies to one's power.

In diametrical opposition to "contemporary bleeding hearts," Nietzsche affirmed that violence and suffering were intrinsic to human experience. "There is no feast without cruelty, as man's entire history attests. Punishment, too, has its festive features."[37] "To speak of right and wrong *per se*," Nietzsche contended, "makes no sense at all. No act of violence, rape, exploitation, destruction, is intrinsically 'unjust,' since life itself is violent, rapacious, exploitative, and destructive and cannot be conceived otherwise."[38] Now, as then, the will to life demanded and justified taking a human life. Nietzsche did not hesitate to draw the least democratic, non-utilitarian, and anti-progressive conclusion: "To sacrifice humanity as a mass to the welfare of a single stronger human species would indeed constitute progress."[39]

Bloody sacrifice, Nietzsche contended, was essential to the spiritual self-definition of archaic peoples. "Early societies were convinced that their continuance was guaranteed solely by the sacrifices and achievements of their ancestors and that these sacrifices and achievements required to be paid back."[40] With this debt acknowledged to their ancestors, who existed in their minds as powerful spirits, "some major act of 'redemption,' some gigantic repayment of the creditor" had to be made to them.⁴¹ Their survival and prosperity depended upon it. In this sense of indebtedness, Nietzsche found a kind of logic which accounted for the creation of more and more powerful ancestors who eventually were transformed into gods. "The fear of the ancestor and his power and the consciousness of his indebtedness increase in direct proportion as the power of the tribe itself increases, as it becomes more and more successful in batttle, independent, respected, and feared. Never the other way around.... Following this kind of logic to its natural terms, we arrive at a situation in which the ancestors of the most powerful tribes have become so fearful to the imagination that they have receded at least into a numinous shadow: *the ancestor becomes a god*. Perhaps this is the way all gods have arisen, out of fear...."⁴²

Nietzsche's conclusions followed: "Just as man has inherited from the blood aristocracies the concepts of good and bad, together with the psychological penchant for hierarchies," so Nietzsche argued a propos the emergence of collective guilt in archaic man, "he had inherited from the tribes, together with the tribal gods, a burden of outstanding debt and the desire to make final restitution."⁴³

If Nietzsche were to succeed in his genealogy of modern conscience, he had to find the "missing links" between the sources of morality he deciphered in archaic man's collective sense of indebtedness, the aristocratic concept of good and bad, and the slave revolt in morality. For Nietzsche, Christianity was the missing link. Within it slave morality and the sense of indebtedness were joined, and created the religion of the sick conscience. Nietzsche wrote: "Then suddenly we come face to face with that paradoxical and ghastly expedient which brought temporary relief to tortured humanity",

> *God's sacrifice of himself for man.* God makes himself the ransom for what could not otherwise be ransomed; God alone has power to absolve us of a debt we can no longer discharge (original sin); the creditor offers himself as a sacrifice for his debtor out of sheer love (can you believe it?) *out of love for his debtor.*⁴⁴

Christianity, Nietzsche defyingly asserted, was the perfect religion for the resentful person. Of his moral logic Nietzsche wrote: All suffering, weakness, miserableness throw him upon his God; all his abnegation and self-denials are understood to win him Heaven. Contrariwise, he sees all who yield to their instincts, flesh, or will, of the Devil, and destined to face judgment and Hell. With Christianity,

Nietzsche asserted, Israel triumphed over classical nobility. The weak and debased took their vengeance against the noble.

Nietzsche asked: "What could equal in debilitating narcotic power the symbol of the "holy cross," the ghastly paradox of a crucified god, the unspeakably cruel mystery of God's self-crucifixion for the benefit of mankind?"[45] "Did not Israel attain the ultimate goal of its sublime vengefulness precisely through the bypath of this 'Redeemer,' this ostensible opponent and disintegrator of Israel?"[46] The Romans, Nietzsche remarked of the "most noble people," succeeded to a degree in counteracting and containing this Jewish-Christian fanaticism through their influence on the Church, but the German Reformation and the English Reformation again brought forward, with all its virulence, this spiritual disease of eternal guilt and everlasting punishment—"this most terrible sickness that has wasted man thus far."[47]

Christianity, for Nietzsche, was based on the hatred of life, with its hopes of a life beyond, its bloody phantasmagoria of the sacrificial animal, the redemptive deed, the holy legend and its asceticism. It, too, was the creator of the new slaves, who had taught equality by virtue of having an everlasting soul.[48]

The French Revolution was, in Nietzsche's opinion, a result of this Christian doctrine of equality. And these new slaves of equality were, in Nietzsche's interpretation, the weak and the resentful; "the maggot man. . . , the 'tame man,' the hopelessly mediocre and insipid man [who] has already learned to feel himself as the goal and zenith, as the meaning of history, as 'higherman.'"[49]

Nietzsche held Christianity to be responsible for more than the prevalent anti-life, "herding-animal morality." Nietzsche judged it to be the teacher of contemporary teachers. From it all those sickly reformers, liberals, democrats, and especially socialists, inherited their faiths—that fetish-like concern for suffering, that fashionable "ethics of pity," that "tragic empathy" for the downtrodden. All this was but a secularized *"la nostalgie de la croix."*[50]

In liberalism, socialism, and democracy, Nietzsche saw the results of Christianity.[51] He described liberals, democrats, and socialists as sharing a mutated Christian faith:

> At one in their tenacious opposition to every special claim, every special right and privilege (this means ultimately opposition to *every* right, for when all are equal, no one needs "rights" any longer); at one in their distrust of punitive justice (as though it were a violation of the weak, unfair to the *necessary* consequences of all former society);

but equally at one in their religion of sympathy, in their compassion for all that feels, lives, and suffers (down to the very animals, up even to "God"–the extravagance of "sympathy, for God" belongs to a democratic age); altogether at one in the cry and impatience of their sympathy, in their deadly hatred of suffering generally, in their almost feminine incapacity for witnessing it or *allowing* it; at one in their involuntary beglooming and heart-softening, under the spell of which Europe seems to be threatened with a new Buddhism; at one in their belief in the morality of *mutual* sympathy, as though it were morality in itself, the climax, the *attained* climax of mankind, the sole hope of the future, the consolation of the present, the great discharge from all the obligations of the past; altogether at one in their belief in the community as the *deliverer*, in the herd, and therefore in "themselves."[52]

Until his absolute mental breakdown in 1890, Nietzsche's life was consumed by his struggle against Christianity. He fought it under the guise of being the prophet Zarathustra, the anti-Christ; with his books, which were titled as banners of his campaigns, *Thus Spake Zarathustra* (1883–1885), *The Anti-Christ* (1888), *The Twilight of the Gods* (1888), *The Gay Science* (1889).

Nietzsche pushed his argumentation to the extremes: Since Christianity had accumulated into itself all past forms of guilt, didn't it follow that a victory over Christianity would be absolute? Wouldn't victory, that is, mean a return to the strong, generous, natural man–a man who gave and took at will? Wouldn't shame, which Nietzsche considered the most vicious, inhuman, and repressing emotion of all, be abolished? Wouldn't innocence, he asked, exist again?

> The advent of the Christian god, . . . has been accompanied by the widest dissemination of the sense of indebtedness, guilt. The steady decline of a belief in a Christian god should entail a commensurate decline in man's guilt consciousness. . . . A complete and definitive victory of atheism might deliver mankind altogether from its feelings of being indebted to its beginnings, its *causa prima*. Atheism and a kind of "second innocence" go together.[53]

At times Nietzsche was ecstatic with hope; victory seemed near. In such a mood Nietzsche wrote the prologue to *Zarathustra*. Zarathustra addresses the people for the first time with these words:

> *I teach you the Superman.* Man is something that is to be surpassed. What have ye done to surpass man? . . .

The Superman is the meaning of the earth. Let your will say: The Superman *shall be* the meaning of the earth!

I conjure you, my brethren, *remain true to the earth*, and believe not those who speak to you of superearthly hopes! Poisoners are they, whether they know it or not.

Despisers of life are they, decaying ones and poisoned ones themselves of whom the earth is weary; so away with them!

Once blasphemy against God was the greatest blasphemy; *but God died*, and therewith also those blasphemers. To blaspheme the earth is now the dreadfulest sin, and to rate the heart of the unknowable higher than the meaning of earth![54]

From the death of God, Nietzsche saw the birth of a new man: a man who is "beyond good and evil," who does what power and spontaneity command, a man of great soul who claims and deserves much."[55] This man, like the greatest heroes of the past, was for Nietzsche the new superman, the Zarathustra, the Dionysus, the new anti-Christ. In Nietzsche's most joyous prophecies, he will be the source of the new order. In his boldest moments, Nietzsche even thought of himself as akin to Christ. He, like some new Christ, would effect an equally great inversion of values.

Nietzsche never escaped the dread of what he sought. "The madman," Nietzsche wrote as if he described himself, "jumped into their midst and pierced them with his eyes. 'Whither is God?' he cried. 'I will tell you. *We have killed him*—you and I. All of us are his murderers.'"[56] The madman told them, murderer of murderers, of the consequences of their deed. For them there was no water or blood to cleanse them, no festival of atonement or rite of purification to relieve them. Only by becoming gods themselves would they have an answer. The madman asked then whether they "heard the burying of God . . . smelled the divine decomposition." He told them that their churches had become "the tombs and sepulchers of God."[57] They did not answer him. The madman's hour had not come.

Nietzsche himself was the madman. He knew that he would die before his "prophecy" was heard. He had carried his offensive against God as far as it could be taken. And still there remained only the certainty of his death. Nietzsche had subjected God to ideas, ideas to history, history to biology and will. If symbols were, as Nietzsche affirmed, but meanings imposed upon our biology and will, then all that is of symbols—the good, the beautiful, the free—can be no more than a seasonal fruit of art, repression, and illusion. Nietzsche insisted that man needs meaning to live: "Man, the most courageous animal and the most inured to trouble, does not deny suffering *per se*, he wants it, he seeks it out, provided it can be given a meaning." "Better the void for a purpose than be void of purpose."⁵⁸

Yet what meaning did Nietzsche leave man? He denied all transcendence to humanity and its suffering. He exhorted man, who was to die, to act as a god.

THE SELF BROKEN AND THE WORLD LOST

Nietzsche's metamorphical, indeed phantasmagorical, transformation of the world was the work of a man separated from the world and divided against himself. Nietzsche's works can justly be read as the story of absolute egoism and the progression of self hate. On the one hand, he increasingly elevated himself to having divine significance. On the other hand, his utter engrossment with himself produced in him a profound self-disgust. At times he depicted himself as an evil man, as the immoralist, as other than human—a beast, the devil, the evil god who attacks all that is valued. However recognizing his own romantic self-dramatization, he turned against himself. He satirized his own ideas, he told the readers of his books and letters not to take him seriously. He posed as a clown, madman, magician. Yet he despised the comedian within himself, for he knew that he was condemned to be deadly serious. Like Dostoevsky's Svidrigailov he asked, "Am I a monster or am I a victim?"⁵⁹ He cast himself in the role of an aristocratic *philosophe* (Voltaire was his favorite), or a cunning French aphorist like La Rochefoucauld, but in truth he was not of those families. He was of the family of those tortured and afflicted Christian moralists like Kierkegaard (whom he resembled but didn't know), Dostoevsky (whom he read at the end of his life and admired), and Pascal, for whom he felt such a strong affinity that he wrote: "one should never forgive Christianity for having destroyed such men as Pascal."⁶⁰

Since playing at being a comedian or aristocrat did not free him from the torments of self-hate, he chose to give his suffering a meaning by making himself a martyr. He intended to make his mind the laboratory of his age. He would bring the world into his mind and there test it. That would give his suffering a value; he would make his self-experiments the way to new truths. His posture was not without similarity to that of those *fin du siècle* anarchists who believed that individual heroic deeds of destruction were steps to a new order. Revealing the identity he made between personal suffering and creative destruction, Nietzsche wrote:

> I know my fate. One day my name will be associated with the memory of something tremendous—a crisis without equal on earth, the most profound collision of conscience, a decision that was conjured up *against* everything that had been believed, demanded, hallowed so far. I am no man. I am dynamite.[61]

Nietzsche hastened to add, thereby exposing the logic of self-hatred which ruled his spirit: "I do not want to be a holy man; sooner even a buffoon. Perhaps I am a buffoon."[62]

Nietzsche's self-hate was inseparable from the condition of his growing isolation. He was without wife or lover. His mother and sister did not afford him a family life. His friendships, never many, dwindled in number and diminished in quality after the rupture of his friendship with composer Wagner and the resignation from his university teaching position in 1876. His works, despite their ever more provocative declarations, brought him only a handful of readers—and they were not the dedicated admirers whom Nietzsche, in his optimistic moments, took them to be. In the 1880s Nietzsche moved from place to place, from boarding home to boarding home. His possessions could be hauled in a single trunk. Obsessed by his ideas, and in the grips of an intensifying hypochondria, Nietzsche ever more desperately pursued his own cure. By reading, writing, medicine, and the constant changing of residences, Nietzsche futilely sought health of body and peace of mind.[63] Madness increasingly settled upon him, and more and more he mistook it for the truth.

In the course of the 1880s Nietzsche came to resemble a Dostoevskyan creature. He was alone, having only his pride and resentment for companions. Like Raskolnikov, the more helpless became, the more he thought of great heroic deeds; and one day in January of 1889, he emerged from his apartment in Turin to see a man beating a horse. He was overwhelmed by the experience. At that point he passed, in psychological terms, from a neurotic to a psychotic state—from anxiety and obsessions to dissociation of self and world.[64]

The depths of disease can be measured by the flow of insane letters he began sending: Aside from friends, he sent letters to such people as King Umberto of Italy and the Vatican Secretary, Mariani. He signed his letters, "The Crucified." In a letter to Strindberg he announced his intention to call a convocation of princes in Rome and to have the young Emperor Wilhelm II shot.[65] He asked his friend Peter Gast: "Sing me a new song: the world is transfigured and all the heavens rejoice."[66]

In what was one of his last letters to his old mentor, Jacob Burckhardt, Nietzsche took himself to be everyone else. He considered himself to be a Parisian murderer then on trial, dead King Vittorio Emmanuele. . . "at the root of every name in history is I."[67] He declared himself to be God: "I go everywhere in my student overcoat; slap someone or other on the shoulder and say: 'Are we happy? I'm God. I made this mess.' ('*Siamo contenti? Son dio, ha fatto questa caricatura*')."[68] His attempts at humor didn't conceal his madness from Burckhardt or Nietzsche's friend, Franz Overbeck. The latter came and got Nietzsche and took him home to his mother and sister. There he lived for the next decade until his death in 1900, never regaining his lucidity. He had lost himself and the world.

However much Nietzsche's madness was uniquely his own, it was also that of this culture. As an intellectual he connected his own personal meaning to the public world. Nietzsche, in fact, could not separate his own significance from that which he attributed to his times. His conceptions of good and bad, life and death, noble and ignoble – the very terms out of which he fashioned his own meaning – became inseparable from the dialogue he carried on with his age. By the end of his career there was nearly nothing left of himself except that stream of judgments he hurled at his age. He had done to a great degree, what all intellectuals and politicians *do to a lesser degree*, and all citizens of a modern nation-state do: *He had made himself his age.*

EGOISM AT ITS EXTREME

One irony of Nietzsche's fate deserves a comment in conclusion. Throughout his writings Nietzsche had consistently made himself the enemy of Rousseau. When he faced that choice between Voltaire or Rousseau, which every student of French letters and modern intellectual history must make, Nietzsche whole-heartedly chose Voltaire, for his attacks against the Church, superstition, and religion. Voltaire was, for Nietzsche, an aristocrat – an expression of the Renaissance sense of *umanità*, a true representative of high culture who fought "for the cause of '*honnêtes gens*' and '*de la bonne compagnie*', the cause of taste, of science, of the arts, of progress itself and civilization."[69] Contrariwise, Rousseau for Nietzsche was *plebian*, a petty *hommes de lettres*, a man filled by "an impudent contempt of all that was not himself." He was "beyond a doubt," Nietzsche contended, "mentally disturbed," marked by *"the rancor of the sick"*: "the periods of his insanity were also those of his contempt of man and his mistrust."[70] Nietzsche held Rousseau, as no other, to be responsible for decadent romanticism, which for Nietzsche had the following characteristics:

"passion ('the sovereign right of passion'); 'naturalness'; the fascination of madness (folly included in greatness); the absurd vanity of the weak man; the rancor of the mob as judge (for a hundred years now, a sick man has been accepted as leader in politics,')."[71] In short, Nietzsche condemned Rousseau as one of the fathers of *"the race moutonnière."*

These stern judgments of Rousseau shared the same plight as so much else in Nietzsche's life. They did not grow out of the tortuous duality of Nietzsche's love-hate relationship with himself. In lucid moments Nietzsche knew his lineage was not of Voltaire, or of his beloved Goethe, but of the Rousseau whom he struggled so hard to despise. The family resemblance was too striking to deny. Both were profoundly in love with themselves. Both spent most of their adult lives without stable relations or a home of their own, and were filled with the sense of being rejected and ignored. Both were profoundly involved with the ideas, values and styles of their age. They took them personally. They were grim and humorless men. They had nearly identical afflictions. They tried to write their way to the peace and the recognition they could never have.

Rousseau and Nietzsche did in excess what all modern people do in measure. They confused themselves with their age. The made their search for themselves equivalent to the search for humanity's meaning.

Nietzsche, chronological son of Rousseau, made egoism cosmic. In the name of the creative self he denied all else – the common good, community, religion, God, as well as the fundamental aspirations of his age, its democracy, its utilitarianism, social reform, socialism, and nationalism. He was a man against his times. Nietzsche would accept none of the era's determinations. Nietzsche recognized neither tradition, nor progress, nor faith in God as being superior to the self. For Nietzsche, the good was the unlimited affirmation of the self.

Nietzsche defied the era's collectivities of nation-states, industrial cities, and mass culture. Nietzsche argued this most radically: "God was dead," and "the hour glass of time was ready to be turned." The new self would do it.

Nietzsche made it seem that self could transcend the gathering forces of his era, as if certain individuals need not share the fate of their times. And, because of this, Nietzsche allows one to convert the world into one's thoughts about it and to feel superior to it for having performed this kind of psychological alchemy. Nietzsche was not stingy. He offered a variety of postures for those who were disenchanted with the world: with the claims of progress, mass culture, and bourgeois consumption. Nietzsche also had an appeal for all those who sense that the new emerging cultures of collectivism are dangerously strong and that the older traditional and aristocratic cultures are terribly weak.

For us, certain questions cannot be avoided: Did Nietzsche, in seeking to escape the illusions of history, god, progress, and contemporary collectivities, betray us to the new illusion of the self—its consciousness, will, and creativity? Is not the self (at least the autonomous self) always an illusion? Is not the self a particular illusion in our era when collectivities rule? However we answer these questions, the self is neither easily defined nor simply made a value in itself, as most doctrines of egoism would have us believe. How precarious the self and reason are in our world was well understood by Henry Adams, the subject of our next chapter.

NOTES

1. See the Bio-Bibliography of Nietzsche at the end of this work.
2. A few useful works to introduce one to the late nineteenth century are E. J. Hobsbawm, *The Age of Capital, 1848-1875* (New York, 1975); Robert Binkley, *Realism and Nationalism, 1852-1871* (New York, 1935); Norman Rich, *The Age of Nationalism, 1850-1890* (New York, 1970); Carlton Hayes, *The Generation of Materialism, 1871-1900* (New York, 1941); Ernst Nolte, *Three Faces of Fascism* (New York, 1966); H. S. Hughes, *Consciousness and Society* (New York, 1961); George Mosse, *The Nationalization of the Masses* (New York, 1975); Fritz Stern, *Politics of Cultural Despair* (New York, 1963); and Eugen Weber, *Peasants into Frenchmen* (Stanford, 1976).
3. Geoffrey Clive, ed., *The Philosophy of Nietzsche* (New York, 1965), 202.
4. Friedrich Nietzsche, *The Will to Power*, trans. Walter Kaufmann (New York, 1968), 42.
5. Friedrich Nietzsche, *The Birth of Tragedy*, trans. Francis Golffing (New York, 1956), 56-57.
6. Friedrich Nietzsche, *Die Geburt der Tragödie, Friedrich Nietzsche, Werke in Zwei Bänden* (Munich, 1967), I, 48.
7. *Birth of Tragedy*, 86.
8. *Ibid.*, 94.
9. This conception of life as a work of art, and its important place in Nietzsche's thought, testifies to the profound influence upon Nietzsche of Swiss cultural historian Jacob Burckhardt; especially influential was Burckhardt's *Civilization of the Renaissance*, 1860.
10. *Birth of Tragedy*, 51.
11. *Ibid.*, 102.
12. *Ibid.*, 52.

13. *Ibid.*, 138.
14. *Ibid.*, 136.
15. *Ibid.*, 137.
16. *Ibid.*, 124.
17. *Ibid.*, 120.
18. Friedrich Nietzsche, *Ecce Homo, Basic Writings of Nietzsche*, ed. Walter Kaufmann, (New York, 1968), 730.
19. Friedrich Nietzsche, *The Use and Abuse of History*, trans. Adrian Collins (New York, 1957), 12.
20. *Ibid.*, 17.
21. *Ibid.*, 3.
22. *Ibid.*, 23.
23. *Ibid.*, 21.
24. *Ibid.*
25. *Ibid.*, 6.
26. *Ibid.*, 9.
27. Friedrich Nietzsche, *The Genealogy of Morals*, trans Francis Golffing (New York, 1956), 217-218.
28. Friedrich Nietzsche, *The Gay Science*, trans. Walter Kaufmann (New York, 1974), 175.
29. *Ibid.*, 176.
30. *Genealogy of Morals*, 173.
31. *Ibid., Basic Writings of Nietzsche*, 472.
32. *Genealogy of Morals*, trans. Francis Golffing, 167.
33. *Ibid.*
34. *Ibid.*, 167.
35. *Ibid.*, 167-168.
36. *Ibid.*, 213.
37. *Ibid.*, 198.
38. *Ibid.*, 208.
39. *Ibid.*, 210.
40. *Ibid.*, 222.
41. *Ibid*
42. *Ibid.*
43. *Ibid.*, 223.
44. *Ibid.*, 225. Emphasis is mine.
45. *Ibid.*, 169.
46. *Genealogy of Morals*, ed. Walter Kaufmann, 471.
47. *Genealogy of Morals*, trans. Francis Golffing, 226.
48. *Will to Power*, 150.
49. *Genealogy of Morals*, ed. Walter Kaufmann, 479.
50. *Genealogy of Morals*, 200.
51. Karl Jaspers, *Nietzsche and Christianity* (Henry Regnery Company, 1961), 39.
52. Clive, *Philosophy of Nietzsche*, 404-405.
53. *Genealogy of Morals*, 224. Emphasis is mine.

54. Friedrich Nietzsche, *Thus Spake Zarathustra*, trans. Thomas Common (New York, n.d.), 6-7.
55. Friedrich Nietzsche, *Beyond Good and Evil, Basic Writings of Nietzsche*, 328.
56. Friedrich Nietzsche, *The Gay Science*, 181.
57. *Ibid.*, 181-182.
58. *Genealogy of Morals*, 298-299.
59. Feodor Dostoevsky, *Crime and Punishment*, trans. Sidney Monas (New York, 1968), 541.
60. *Will To Power*, 145.
61. Friedrich Nietzsche, *Ecce Homo, Basic Writings of Nietzsche*, 782.
62. *Ibid.* Nietzsche knew from Burckhardt's *Civilization of the Renaissance* that bid for greatness was a reason for satire, and even a path to folly.
63. No single essay so well develops the pathos of Nietzsche's last years as Stefan Zweig's lengthy piece on Nietzsche, "A One-Man Drama," *Master Builders* (New York, 1939), 443-530.
64. Christopher Middleton has selected, translated, and prepared a fine collection of Nietzsche's letters, *Selected Letters of Nietzsche* (Chicago, 1969).
65. *Ibid.*, 344.
66. *Ibid.*, 345.
67. *Ibid.*, 347.
68. *Ibid.*, 348.
69. *Will To Power*, 63.
70. *Ibid.*
71. *Ibid.*, 64.

CHAPTER FIVE

Henry Adams: An Angry Patrician, Before Power Beyond Measure

IN THE LAST THIRD of the nineteenth century, the West radiated power in all directions. No single term—urbanization, industrialization, colonization, Westernization, or modernization—is adequate to comprehend the power humanity unleashed upon the world.[1] Seas, mountains, jungles, deserts, animals, which had been unaltered since time immemorial, felt the intrusion of this power. In some cases this power annihilated what it touched; in other cases governments granted temporary stays to an area, an animal species, or tribe, by assigning them the status of park, wilderness, or reservation.

In this period Western man took control of society and nature. Some intellectuals found reason for hope in this great power. They rallied around the promise of reform, revolution, democracy, and progress, dreaming of a glorified humanity. Other intellectuals found no hope in man's accumulating power. They despaired of progress.[2] The most extreme of these pessimists spoke of the inevitability of conflict, hungered for cultures and pasts with almost a violent nostalgia, or fled the West, its cities and materialism for the supposed simplicity, spirituality, or sheer exotic character of distant lands. The loss of community was the standard plaint of the hour. (In fact, Émile Durkheim and Max Weber gave birth to modern sociology around the theme of the loss of community to the rationalizing processes of modern law, bureaucratization, and state.)

Difficult as it is to imagine a more pessimistic reaction to the era than Nietzsche's, the reaction of Henry Adams was. Adams (1838-1918) was a grand patrician. He was of the Adams family which had furnished two presidents to the United States. His family not only lived by the philosophy of eighteenth century rational humanism, but they had helped fashion it.[3] Like Nietzsche, Adams saw his own age dominated by coarse and vulgar forces. But unlike Nietzsche, Adams did not see the contemporary world's condition being essentially a matter of cultural decadence; nor did he believe there was in nature or spirit the possibility of rebirth. For Adams, history followed no circle of birth, death, and rebirth. For Adams, history was irreversibly linear, propelled forward at ever greater speeds by ever more impersonal forces.

Adams' view raised the most elemental ethical questions: Does man create forces and institutions which he cannot control? If so, what is his ethical responsibility for them? How does man order his public life if it is in bondage to impersonal forces? What is the relation of the public world's realities to the values of one's private life; i.e., those of person, family, and religion? Finally, what values can remain if the public world is antithetical to all values?

These questions increasingly became Adams' anguish, and his anguish became his life. Unable to find the career he deserved by right of family tradition and education, Adams turned away from the public world. Suffering the suicide of the woman who provided him a shelter in a world of few havens, Adams was left without intimate center. Adams became a solitary, lonely man; in a sense, he became sheer mind. He was driven by the singular obsession to understand the meaning of an age whose complexity and anarchy he knew to defy all human comprehension. This was the paradox, the irony, and genius of this American Nietzsche, this solitary patrician who uniquely suffered the radical change which was making his era into our own.[4]

A PATRICIAN, WITHOUT PLACE OR LOYALTY

As no other intellectual in this period had, Henry Adams—journalist, historian, writer, member of the Adams family—confronted the intensification of human power. In his best-known works he grappled with it.

In *Mont-Saint-Michel and Chartres* (1904), he drew a powerful contrast between the Middle Ages and his own times. Medieval man was subject to the Virgin's rule; as an idea-force, she ruled. Adams believed that contemporary man, in contrast to medieval man, was without a symbol to join his earthly condition and eternal hopes. His only symbol would be the dynamo, which in fact was no symbol at all. It expressed simply the reality of man's accumulating power. The dynamo didn't join heaven and earth. It couldn't be prayed to. The only truth of the dynamo was: more power, more complexity, more multiplicity—and eventually, chaos.

In Adams' pessimistic view, contemporary man was without a science to understand, a culture to judge, or a politics to guide his power. Power took away old faiths and brought new terrors. It was taking man beyond good and evil as he knew them.

In "The Rule of Phase Applied to History" (1909), Adams (inspired by Comte's evolutionary view of history and his brother Brooks' pessimistic science of mass democracy) proposed this terrifying development of human history vis-à-vis power.

> There was first the era of instinct, a long epoch in which men were controlled by purely automatic drives. The era of instinct was succeeded, after thousands of years, by the era of religion. . . . As the power of religion waned, man's fate came to be controlled increasingly by mechanical forces, and the mechanical period was succeeded, in turn, by the electrical period, whose symbol was the dynamo. With the twentieth century—more specifically the discovery of radium—came the impact of "supersensual forces."[5]

Adams wrote of the new power:

> The world did not double or triple its movement between 1800 and 1900, but, measured by any standard known to science—by horsepower, calories, volts, mass in any shape—the tension and vibration and volume and so-called progression of society were fully a thousand times greater in 1900 than in 1800;—the force had doubled ten times over, and the speed, when measured by electrical standards as in telegraphy, approached infinity, and had annihilated both space and time. No law of material movement applied to it.[6]

Adams believed that "science is wrecking man," that "man could not hold off such forces."[7] He wrote in 1902 that it seemed "mathematically certain that another thirty years of energy-development at the rate of the last century must reach an *impasse*."[8] This prophecy missed the atomic bombing of Hiroshima and Nagasaki by thirteen years.

The dominating theme of Adams' partially autobiographical classic, *Education* (1906, though not published until shortly after his death in 1918), was his encounter with power. He perceived it in that radical growth of financial, commercial, industrial, and imperial empires which marked the last half of the nineteenth century. He saw it taking form in the vast range of new scientific discoveries and inventions which dominated the period. (The new chemistry and physics of the atom were of particular importance to Adams.) After ten years of seeking to understand the new forces of his era, Adams "found himself lying in the Gallery of Machines at the Great Exposition of 1900, his historical neck broken by the sudden eruption of forces totally new."[9] Adams described this revolution in these terms: "Copernicus and Galileo had broken many professional necks about 1600; Columbus had stood the world on its head towards 1500; but the nearest approach to the revolution of 1900 was that of 310, when Constantine set up the Cross."[10]

The title *Education* served Adams' ironic purposes. The aim of his work was to understand what was incomprehensible. He argued that his "education" only led him to find "no paradox compared with that of daily events. *The facts were constantly outrunning his thoughts.*"[11]

Education that had startled and invigorated his youth wearied him in old age: "To educate — one's self to begin with — had been the effort of one's life for sixty years; and the difficulties of education had gone on doubling with the coal output, until the prospect of waiting another ten years, in order to face a seventh doubling of complexities, allured one's imagination but slightly."[12]

Adams made the implication of his education universal. Optimistically he wrote: "At the rate of progress since 1800, every American who lived into the years 2000 would know how to control unlimited power. He would think complexities unimaginable to an earlier mind. . . . To him the nineteenth century would stand on the same plane with the fourth — equally childlike."[13] However, ahead for mankind, Adams asserted, was a mortal leap: "The movement from unity into multiplicity, between 1200 and 1900, was unbroken in sequence, and rapid in acceleration. Prolonged from one generation longer, it would require a new social mind. . . . Thus far, since five or ten thousand years, the mind had successfully reacted, and nothing yet proved that it would fail to react — but it would need to jump."[14]

Adams' life was not ordinary. By birth alone his biography and education were certain to have an historical significance. This was so because he was an Adams. The most modest history of his family was, in measure, a history of the United States. If there had been an American aristocracy, Adams not only would have belonged to it, but defined it. If anyone were to presume an identity between private life and public world, it would have been Adams. Henry Adams' great-grandfather, John Adams, was second president of the United States; his grandfather, John Quincy Adams, who helped raise Henry at the homestead in Quincy, was sixth president of the United States; and Henry's father, Charles Francis Adams, lawyer and diplomat, was a founder of the Free Soil Party, a candidate for vice-President of the United States, and served the most important ambassadorial post in nineteenth century America: he was United States ambassador to England during the Civil War. His birth not only entitled him to acquaintances with those who made American history, but his education was intended to prepare him to do the same. After an education at Harvard, he studied in Germany, traveled throughout Europe, and served as secretary in the London consulate for his father. Already, while still a young man, Adams had come to know the American and European aristocracies.

It was inevitable that Adams' education put him on a collision course with his times. Adams' presumption belonged to another age. "It was not possible," Vernon Parrington wrote, "for the House of Adams, with its old-fashioned rectitude, to accept the ways of the Gilded Age, and in the end they turned aside from the main-traveled road to follow their own paths."[15] Bert Loewenberg offers other reasons why Adams would not be at home in the new industrial America which took form after the Civil War:

> He eschewed the major lines of force of his own society perhaps because he was an Adams, or perhaps, being an Adams, he was incapable of coming to terms with the kind of world it was. He abjured power by means of wealth. Adams had sufficient financial resources to do what he wanted, but he was no nabob. The nabobs of the gilded age repelled him, and Adams rarely lost the chance to scoff at money and the men who made it—although he was free from financial cares because of those who made it for him and those who administered it afterwards. He likewise abjured power by means of the Adams standing and the Adams name. While he detested the new society and its materialistic standards, he resented the indifference of the new society to the Adams values and the Adams heritage. None could deliberately ignore an Adams, but the lords of steel and the barons of coal were impervious to his existence. The difference between the House of Adams and the House of Morgan was the difference between two centuries of American history. President Grant, as far as Henry Adams was concerned, may have been enough to upset Darwin, but it was U. S. Grant, not Charles Francis Adams—nor indeed Henry Brooks Adams—who sat in the White House.[16]

It was preordained that Adams should voice reaction. He was an aristocrat in an age of the emerging masses.[17] His hatred of the new materialisms, mass cities, as well as bankers, was never concealed. Although Adams did not engage in a politics of nostalgia, which nurtured hopes of restoring the old order, he shared traditional American intellectual distrust of the city, the machine, and the urban masses. Adams consistently showed himself to be indifferent to the masses; their welfare, public health, and education had no place in his writing. His concerns were elitist. Culture, political leadership, and individual conscience were the first issues of his *Education*.

Adams' *Education*, however, was more than class reaction. It was more than a self-pitying tale of his failure to take up a career in a world which he was born to rule. Adams used his failed careers to speak of man's growing power and deepening ignorance.

Adams' first career was his diplomatic service with his father in England during the Civil War. It instructed him in the deceitful intricacies of the diplomats' dark craft: its truths are rarely what they appear to be. Misunderstanding and deception are warp and woof of its creations. Its actions are seldom understood by its actors.

Back in the United States, Adams tried his hand at journalism in Grant's Washington. Aside from learning of journalism's impotence, Adams got his primary education in domestic politics. Adams now had "to admit that nine-tenths of his acquired education was useless, and the other tenth harmful."[18] "Politics," Adams wrote of what he discovered in Washington, "had ceased to disturb social relations. All parties were mixed up and jumbled together in a sort of tidal slackwater. The government resembled Adams himself in the matter of education. All that had gone before was useless, and some of it was worse."[19]

Adams saw his own inheritance slated for extinction: "The progress of evolution from President Washington to President Grant, was alone enough to upset Darwin. . . . America had no use for Adams because he was eighteenth century, and yet it worshipped Grant because he was archaic, and should have lived in a cave and worn skins."[20] From Grant's regime nothing could be learned, Adams argued. "Education became more perplexing at every phase. No theory was worth the pen that wrote it."[21] "Darwinists," Adams chided, "ought to conclude that America was reverting to the stone age, but the theory of reversion was more absurd than that of evolution. Grant's administration reverted to nothing. One could not catch a trait of the past, still less of the future."[22] Adams, "all of whose hopes of success in life turned on his finding an administration to support," left Washington, disappointed, without a cause.[23] "All he wanted was something to support; something that would let itself be supported. Luck went dead against him. For once, he was fifty years in advance of his time."²⁴

Adams accepted the call to Harvard, his alma mater, in 1871, to take up the post of medieval history, a subject with which he had no acquaintance whatsoever. Nevertheless, he reasoned, he knew as much about twelfth century Paris as he did contemporary America. Perhaps quiet and books would heal his wounds.

There were the wounds of the public life – those Augean stables of post-Civil War politics, which would require a Herculean patrician to spend a life-time of energy to clean them of that filth, ruin, and corruption. Confessing his pessimism, Adams wrote, this world "cared little for decency"; "the moral world had expired – like the Constitution."²⁵ Abroad there was the hurt of the Franco-Prussian War of 1870: "Providence set no affiches to announce the tragedy. Under one's eyes France cut herself adrift, and floated off, on an unknown stream, towards a less known ocean."²⁶ Also, in 1870, his sister died. Her death taught Adams that nature savagely kills, and that God is indifferent to its violence. Adams described "this last lesson – the sum and term of education":

> He had never seen Nature – only her surface – the sugarcoating that she shows to youth. Flung suddenly in his face, with the harsh brutality of chance, the terror of the blow stayed by him thenceforth for life, until repetition made it more than the will could struggle with; more than he could call on himself to bear. He found his sister, a woman of forty, as gay and brilliant in the terrors of lockjaw as she had been in the careless fun of 1859, lying in bed in consequence of a miserable cab-accident that had bruised her foot. Hour by hour the muscles grew rigid, while the mind remained bright, until after ten days of fiendish torture, she died in convulsions.²⁷

Up to then, Adams said, he lived by the customs and masks provided by "immortal society." Now he was stripped naked, ripped open as he endured a ten-day death-vigil, during which there was nothing to do but watch Nature on that picturesque and delightful Tuscan stage, "torture and smother his sister with caresses. . . . For many thousand years on these hills and plains, Nature had gone on sabering men and women with the same air of sensual pleasure."²⁸ Nature became for Adams a violently insane force which science and religion neither explained nor mollified. To Adams defiance alone seemed honorable; God must be rejected. Adams wrote:

> For the first time, the stage-scenery of the senses collapsed; the human mind felt itself stripped naked, vibrating in a void of

shapeless energies, with resistless mass, colliding, crushing, wasting, and destroying what these same energies had created and labored from eternity to perfect. Society became fantastic, a vision of pantomime with a mechanical motion; and its so-called thought merged in the mere sense of life, and pleasure in the sense. The usual anodynes of social medicine became evident artifice. Stoicism was perhaps the best; religion was the most human; but the idea that any personal deity could find pleasure or profit in torturing a poor woman, by accident, with a fiendish cruelty known to man only in perverted and insane temperaments, could not be held for a moment. For pure blasphemy, it made pure atheism a comfort. God might be, as the Church said, a Substance, but He could not be a Person.[29]

Adams did what he could at Harvard to heal his wounds. He made friends with fellow faculty, James Russell Lowell, Francis J. Child, Louis Agassiz, his son Alexander, Gurney, John Fiske, William James, and others. But these best educated and most sociable men in America could not break out of their isolation as professors. The society which they formed at Cambridge made "a social desert that would have starved a polar bear."

If there was anything of worth holding Adams at Harvard, it was with the students. Starting with the candid recognition that he did not know the subject he was asked to teach, he denied the worth of the general lecture hall. Adams invited his students into small seminars. There they would explore the Middle Ages together. Adams believed that it was understanding, not knowledge, that mattered.

After six years at Harvard, his popularity and success as a teacher acclaimed, Adams drew the conclusion he had nothing to teach youth. His discipline, history, "had lost even the sense of shame. It was a hundred years behind the experimental sciences. For all serious purposes, it was less instructive than Walter Scott and Alexandre Dumas."[30] He saw no way of escaping the choice of either treating "history as a catalogue, a record, a romance, or as an evolution; and whether he affirms or denies evolution, he falls into all the burning faggots of the pit. He makes of his scholars either priests or atheists, plutocrats or socialists, judges or anarchists, almost in spite of himself. *In essence incoherent and immoral history had to be taught as such—or falsified.*"[31] Adams saw no way to offer those students—who wanted a Harvard degree for better reasons than making money in Chicago—an education that would "lessen the obstacles, diminish the friction, invigorate the energy, and should train their minds to react, not at haphazard, but by choice, on the lines of forces that attract their world."[32]

Leaving Harvard to edit the *North American Review*, he remarked:

"Thus it turned out that of all his many educations, Adams thought that of school teacher the thinnest. Yet he was forced to admit that the education of an editor, in some ways, was thinner still."³³ "A professor," Adams noted, "had at least the pleasure of associating with his students; an editor lived the life of an owl. A professor commonly became a pedagogue or a pedant; an editor became an authority on advertising."³⁴ The editorship, however, introduced Adams to everyone who was writing anything, and he was again tempted to test his wit and conscience against a radically changing America.

Adams chose to omit from the *Education* the years 1877-1890. He titled his chapter after the Harvard teaching experience "Twenty Years After." He made 1890 the counter-point of 1870: "Education had ended in 1871; life was complete in 1890; the rest mattered so little."³⁵ His generation (made up of William Phillips, Bret Harte, Henry James, H. H. Richardson, as well as his close friends Clarence King, John La Farge, and John Hay) had become what they could; their adventure had found its highest trajectory. All that was waited for was its descent. "In the year of 1871, the West was still fresh, and the Union Pacific was young. Beyond the Missouri River, one felt the atmosphere of Indians and buffaloes."³⁶ Now, as Frederick Jackson Turner noted in his historic 1893 address, the frontier, the great safety valve of American democracy, was closed. The symbol of America's youth and the possibility of its perpetual renewal was gone. *"No New World to Mankind Remains!"* ran a familiar American poetic lament, which expressed Adams' point of view.³⁷

For Adams, America had joined Europe. Both were now old, overrun by ugly masses, giant cities, and greedy bankers. Adams shared the artists' stylish hate of the culturally pretentious bourgeois. He found no cause with labor or in the amelioration of the condition of the newly arrived immigrants as did fellow patrician Jane Addams.

Adams found no promise in democracy, no hope in progress. He claimed that he hated the present as much as the anarchists. He wished that Marx was somehow correct. "One revelled at will in the ruin of every society in the past, and rejoiced in proving the prospective overthrow of every society that seemed possible in the future. But meanwhile, these societies which violated every law—moral, arithmetical, and economical—not only propagated each other, but produced also fresh complexities with every propagation and developed mass with every complexity."³⁸

To Adams the America of 1890 denied everything about the republic of his eighteenth century ancestors. The cord was cut. His inheritance was insufficient to the hour. The values of the Enlightenment, its humanities, reason, and conscience, proved to be puny before the forces moving this "New America." America was without a culture, a *paideia*, to give its citizens a way to value and to order life. Only the foolish could any longer maintain the charade of pretending to be members of the Republic. Adams knew that he, like all Americans, "was wandering in a wilderness much more sandy than the Hebrews had ever trodden about in Sinai; they had neither serpent nor golden calves to worship."[39] Not only did the American mind run less towards the pursuit of money than its European counterpart, but it also, Adams contended, "shunned, distrusted, disliked the dangerous attraction of ideals, and stood alone in history for its ignorance of the past."[40]

Adams' near bankruptcy in the 1893 Depression intensified his bitter assessments of America. It helped to assure his reaction to the Chicago Exposition of that year. He responded to it as Dostoevsky had to the Crystal Palace four decades before. It convinced him that future societies would have no place for the individual. Ahead Adams saw the age of the machine, statistics, and the engineers. Past *wisdom* was surpassed; conscience and ethics were antiquated. Even "the artist [in him] began to die; only a certain intense cerebral restlessness survived which no longer responded to sensual stimulants; one was driven to beauty as though art were a trotting match."[41] Unless his irony hid it, Adams had not found a faith to blunt his anguish and skepticism. After 1890, there remained for him only the lonely pursuit of an education which was already botched, futile by its very goal:

> The object of education, therefore, was changed. For many years it had lost itself in studying what the world had ceased to care for ; if it were to begin again, it must try to find out what the mass of mankind did care for, and why. Religion, politics, statistics, and travel had thus far led to nothing. Even the Chicago Fair had only confused the roads. Accidental education could go no further, for one's mind was already littered and stuffed beyond hope with the millions of chance images stored away without order in the memory. *One might as well try to educate a gravelpit*. The task was futile, which disturbed a student less than the discovery that, in pursuing it, he was becoming himself ridiculous. Nothing is more tiresome than a superannuated pedagogue.[42]

With resignation, yet also with a tenacity bordering on the perverse, Adams concluded that the truth could only be found in understanding the lines of force controlling his age. As Adams recognized, he was trying to overtake a reality which was receding as rapidly as he approached it. He was on foot, it was on bicycle; he was on bicycle, it was on train; he was on train, it was in a plane. The chase annihilated consciousness. Adams' feelings wanted explosion; his tradition counseled dogged pursuit, however futile it already had absolutely proven itself to be.

Adams chose irony instead of agony to bear his plight. He would pursue knowledge of a power which was less and less subject to human understanding, value, and control. Adams' constant travels, his engaging friendships, his ironic comportment, and aristocratic demeanor, did not hide his futile struggle to wrench significance out of the maddening flux of things.

By skipping over the 1880s, Adams avoided giving us a full personal accounting of the factors that made him sheer mind more so than any one else in his generation. The first half of the 1880s had been Adams' best decade. Adams and his wife Marian had been happily married for over a decade. Their days were full. They had built a house for themselves in Washington. Around it they formed a circle of friends. To them came not only old acquaintances from all over America and Europe, but "the luminaries and the powers" who made the world what it was. Adams and his wife, in effect, had what affection, what civility, and what knowledge the hour gave.

Adams was productive in these years. It was as if his life had come together, found its proper gait. Marriage, Marian, things were in order. Adams was in a creative period. A steady and varied stream of writing flowed from Adams after his resignation as editor of the *North American Review* in 1877. In 1876 there were the *Essays on Anglo-Saxon Law. Documents Relating to New England Federalism* appeared the following years. And in 1879 his *Life of Albert Gallatin* and his three-volume *Writings of Albert Gallatin* were published. His biographies of Aaron Burr and John Randolph soon followed. Under pen name, Adams tried his hand at social-psychological novels, publishing *Democracy* in 1882 and *Esther* in 1884. At the same time, Adams already had begun to work in earnest on his multi-volume *History of the United States* (the ninth and last volume appeared in 1890), which in the words of one critic, "is the masterwork of his maturity and possibly the finest American contribution to scientific history in the nineteenth century."[43] Focusing on the Jefferson and Madison administrations, Adams sought to take the measure of the breadth and power of the United States in the early 1800s.

At that time Adams was blessed. He had friendship, economic security, pleasure in his work, and a sensitive and loving wife. However, her suicide in December, 1885, cut his life in two. (The causes of her suicide were not entirely clear. She could not overcome the weakness and depression that had settled upon her after her extended care of her dying father. Mental anxiety had always been her problem). The consequences of her suicide for Adams were all too painfully clear. He was again alone in the world. His friends the Camerons, the Hays, the Kings, and others could comfort, but not heal him. He was alone and hurt. Constant travel, continuous thought, and the state of being at war with his times—conditions so common to the mature Nietzsche—became the essence of Adams' way. There was no longer woman, house, a point of intimacy to tether the spirit of this solitary patrician. He became savage in his cerebral assaults against the modern world.

Now, even more than before, Adams took the measure of existence through women's eyes.[44] Already in his *Esther* and *Democracy* he had done this. The heroines of both works share the same dilemma: whether to enter into a marriage that entailed sacrificing the integrity of her conscience to the unfair, immoral demands of a society controlled by men. In *Democracy*, the heroine's crisis centered around the choice of marrying an unscrupulous politician. In *Esther*, marriage means for the heroine the acceptance of her fiancé's high, intelligent, and fashionable Episcopalianism, at the expense of her own intellectual skepticism. Both heroines decline marriage. Conscience painfully triumphs over love, leaving them with a less than complete life as the reward of their victory. Surely the forceful contradictions explored in these novels pushed Marian towards suicide.

Marian's suicide intensified Adams' growing tendency to make the condition of woman the measure of existence. From her Adams measured the viability of the private world, the morality of the public world, and the possibility of divine kindness. If intelligence was one measure and his ancestor's republic another, woman was the final measure. She served Adams, as the superman did Nietzsche.

For Adams, woman revealed the accelerating change of modern history. He wrote in the *Education* that in order to keep up an average speed of forty miles an hour, tending always to become sixty, eighty, or a hundred, . . . (the male) could not admit emotions or anxieties or subconscious distractions more than he could admit whiskey or drugs, without breaking his neck. He could not run his machine and a woman too."[45] Her fate was to run after him, to find her own way. Without church she had no refuge.

> She was free; she had no illusions; she was sexless; she had discarded all that the male disliked; and although she secretly regretted the

discard, she knew that she could not go backward. She must, like the man, marry machinery.[46]

The woman for Adams was the territory of the perennial and the intimate. She was the force of resistance, the *vis inertiae*, the continuity—the center which gave unity to life. Yet she, in her *avant-garde* American form, was coming undone. She, too, was being subject to the forces of change. Insecure in home, body, and spirit, she was set to running. Anxiety, frenzy, and the sense of absence they produce filled her with the guilt of not being any longer, as she once was, the victim of man and church; she was now becoming the victim of the machine. The forces which were transforming the world, reaching to the most remote territories of Russia and Asia, reached woman herself: Something elemental was changing. Adams' horror before this change led him to write: "One was almost glad to act the part of horseshoe crab in Quincy Bay, and admit that all was uniform—that nothing ever changed—and that the woman would swim about the ocean of future time, as she had swum in the past, with the gar fish and the shark, unable to change."[47]

The change which had overrun his father's Republic was now undoing motherhood itself. A revolution, far more profound than Darwin's evolution, was occurring. This explains Adams' attraction to the Virgin. The Virgin Mary was the great mother of pity. Like the suffering and forgiving woman of Dostoevsky, the Virgin for Adams meant the existence of answers in an impersonal universe. She was love in a world of forces. She was the remnant of the ethical in an amoral world. Adams had reason to envy those Catholics whose belief in Mary gave them hope that beyond the bitter reciprocities of this life, there was a mother of mercy. Adams understood *how much more man needed mercy than progress!*

Adams knew that the Virgin once concentrated in herself the power of a whole age. "Symbol of energy, the Virgin had acted as the greatest force the Western world had ever felt, and had drawn man's activities to herself more strongly than any other power, natural or supernatural, had ever done."[48] In her name, Adams knew, the peasants sowed their fields, chartered their guilds, raised their greatest monuments, the cathedrals whose stone and glass spoke of man's basic needs and ultimate hopes. The Virgin was, for the medieval person, the hope that existence was ultimately personal.

She was a much more personal symbol than any modern symbol was. She could speak to hearts as Descartes, Hume, Berkeley, Kant, Hegel, and Hartmann, could not.[49] She could harness the blind powers which ruled man as the secular visions of Adams' eighteenth century ancestors could not. She offered a more elemental inspiration than did the republic. She joined love and truth, mother and God.

For Adams she was now only a historical vestige. Perhaps Adams was too Protestant, too secular, or too rational to lend her credence. Perhaps he could not forgive her for his sister's death and his wife's death. Whatever the case Adams was condemned to think instead of to pray. The dynamo drowned out all else, and he could only feel its relentless power pushing him, his forefather's republic, and all humanity towards a land where there was no woman – not even the Virgin in the sky – who could make a home for man.

THE MEASURE OF EVENTS

Of all Henry Adams' contemporaries, none more quickly comes to mind for comparison than Friedrich Nietzsche. Both are isolated men; both are high cultural critics of mass industrial society. They each made desperate efforts to understand their ages. Both repudiated progress, finding what hope they did for mankind in a fundamental transformation of human myths.

Their differences, however, were equally great. Whereas Adams' realism about power produced ironic detachment, Nietzsche remained forever a combative, aggressive romantic. Nietzsche's most positive metaphors were exaggeratedly masculine. They clustered around notions of struggle, will, and power. In contrast to Adams, Nietzsche attacked all that he associated with the feminine; passivity, pity, and love elicited his most vicious criticism. Nietzsche never married, or seemed to have any sustained positive relation with a woman.

Aside from having a gentility and appreciation of the feminine, which Nietzsche did not, Adams understood power. He understood power as it was practiced by politicians and statesmen. By birth and education Adams was instructed in the world's political realities. Nietzsche, on the contrary, had no such political inheritance. His traditional education in the classics only made his isolation from the public world more profound.

Adams and Nietzsche did share a common plight, which is also ours. They tried to bring the essential premises of Enlightenment rationalism to a world marked by the emergence of mass culture and national societies. Mutually they asked what visions would guide the new forces of their era and mutually they concluded that progress was not the answer.

World War I made Adams and Nietzsche prophets. Meaning would have to be struggled for amidst events. The good became an issue of combat.

Mounier, Camus, and Sartre, the three twentieth century intellectuals whom we now go on to explore, each sought the good in a proper attitude about action. Each of them saw the good as a matter of willingness to act on behalf of man, not out of promise of his victory but as the minimal condition of human dignity.

The student of ethics cannot escape asking what is our responsibility to our times. What responsibility do we have to the complex and changing public world? Adams had raised this most fundamental question. Mounier, Camus, and Sartre strove to give it an answer.

NOTES

1. For one suggestive account of the scale of modernization, see Cyril Black, *Dynamics of Modernization* (N.Y., 1968); for the impact of modernization and consciousness see Peter Berger, Brigitte Berger and Hanfried Kellner's *The Homeless Mind* (New York, 1973).

2. One useful survey of this period is H. S. Hughes, *Consciousness and Society* (New York, 1961); also of use is the second chapter of my *Mounier and Maritain*, 29-54.

3. For general approach to Adams' work and writing, see the Bio-Bibliography at the end of this work.

4. The great American cultural critic Lewis Mumford, who wrote pioneering work on the history of the city and technology in the 1930s, came to appreciate Adams in the aftermath of the Second World War.

5. This summary is offered by Henry Commager in his *American Mind* (New Haven, 1950), 287.

6. Henry Adams, "The Rule of Phase Applied to History," *A Henry Adams Reader*, ed. Elizabeth Stevenson (Garden City, N.Y., 1954), 376-77.

7. Cited in Commager, *American Mind*, 287.

8. *Ibid.*

9. Henry Adams, *Education* (New York, 1931), 382.

10. *Ibid.*, 383.

11. *Ibid.*, 339. Emphasis is mine.

12. *Ibid.*, 498.

13. *Ibid.*, 496-497.

14. *Ibid.*, 498.

15. Vernon Louis Parrington, *Main Currents in American Thought, Vol. III, The Beginnings of Critical Realism in America, 1860-1920* (New York, 1930), 213.

16. Bert Loewenberg, *American History in American Thought* (New York, 1972), 543.

17. Similarities exist between Adams' *Education* and Thomas Mann's 1901 novel, *Buddenbrooks*. The latter, too, is the story of displaced patrician grandchildren. Although in this case, it is not that the world has grown more base, ferocious, complex, and confusing, but the children themselves have become too weak and aesthetic to carry on duties of surviving in the real world.
18. Adams, *The Education*, 253.
19. *Ibid.*, 254.
20. *Ibid.*, 266.
21. *Ibid.*
22. *Ibid.*
23. *Ibid.*, 267.
24. *Ibid.*
25. *Ibid.*, 280.
26. *Ibid.*, 290.
27. *Ibid.*, 287.
28. *Ibid.*, 288.
29. *Ibid.*, 289.
30. *Ibid.*, 301.
31. *Ibid.*, 300-301. Emphasis is mine.
32. *Ibid.*, 314.
33. *Ibid.*, 307.
34. *Ibid.*, 308.
35. *Ibid.*, 318.
36. *Ibid.*, 309.
37. This lament declaring the end of pristine America is cited in Henry Nash Smith's *Virgin Land: The American West As Symbol and Myth* (Cambridge, Mass., 1950), 210.
38. Adams, *Education,* 351-352.
39. *Ibid.*, 328.
40. *Ibid.*
41. *Ibid.*, 351.
42. *Ibid.*, 352-353.
43. Cited in Milton Cantor's Introduction, Adams' *John Randolph* (New York, 1961), ix.
44. A useful discussion of Adams' view of contemporary women is found in Ernest Samuel's Introduction to *Democracy and Esther* (Garden City, New York, 1961), xi-xix.
45. Adams, *Education,* 445.
46. *Ibid.*, 447. Emphasis is mine.
47. *Ibid.*, 448.
48. *Ibid.*, 388-389.
49. *Ibid.*, 431-432.

CHAPTER SIX

Emmanuel Mounier: Personalism, a Christian Ethics for Our Times[1]

HENRY ADAMS HAD A TERRIFYING VIEW of history: man had created historical forces that he could neither comprehend nor value. There was only force; no ethics remained. What Adams prophesied seemed to come true the year of his death, 1917.

World War I entered its third awful year. The United States entered the war to break the stalemate; Russia fell to revolution. The nation-states universally mobilized all men, materials, and ideas for the sake of victory. Violence, death, and destruction grew as nation-states and technologies, once thought to be engines of progress, drowned civilization in blood.[2] They were Frankensteins.

The only principle of states at war was victory. And where victory alone counts, values are banished.

The events of 1929-1933 made the worst teachings of the Great World War emphatic. Announced by the Depression in 1929 and culminated by the ascendancy of Hitler to power in Germany in January, 1933, the events of this period taught that liberal-capitalism was in absolute disarray; that democracy was no longer the commanding form of government; that totalitarian statism was emerging, and that pacific internationalism, embodied in the League of Nations, lacked the ability to assure peace. The great hopes of the nineteenth century were in shambles.

Of this period, 1929-1933, Pierre Renouvin wrote:

> By its amplitude and its duration it is without precedent in the contemporary world.... The shaking was so grave and so prolonged that the basis of the economic and social order appeared threatened. Individualism, free enterprise, the setting of prices by competition—the foundations of the capitalist system—were in rout.... It was not thus only an economic and social crisis, and even a moral crisis; it was a

crisis of the collective mind. . . . The *Annus terribilis*, which Arnold Toynbee evoked at the beginning of 1932, was not 1914 or 1917, it was 1931.[3]

As the Great War divided European cultural life by giving license to the most extreme thoughts, so the events of the 1929-1933 period made the gloomiest prophecies and the darkest pessimisms common modes of intellectual discourse.[4] Faith in progress, and its associated trinity of reason, science, and democracy, waned; despair, irrationalism, and blind activism took control.

This "mood" of cosmic questioning transformed itself into an intellectual anxiety over the destiny of man. The increasing importance of the psychologies of Freud and Jung for European intellectual life, no less than the ever-growing number of supporters of Dostoevsky and Nietzsche, were symptomatic of a culture in crisis. Man himself was called into question. This existential anxiety over man and the West transformed and universalized nineteenth century criticisms of bourgeois society and politics. No past criticism of European life went unvoiced; almost all past attacks against European society and culture were taken to be true of the contemporary order.

Emmanuel Mounier (1905-1950) was one intellectual who responded to this crisis. Mounier's response involved two facets: he was French and he was Catholic. To be French meant the paradoxical task of assuming, on the one hand, that one spoke for all of humanity, and on the other hand, it meant increasingly realizing that one's nation held a diminished place in the world.[5]

To be Catholic raised for Mounier the questions that most formed his thought.[6] As a member of a church which claimed to be universal, Mounier asked: How could the Church not be relevant to the world's affairs? Did not the command to imitate Christ, at least for a progressive Catholic like Mounier, carry with it a responsibility to be willing to enter into the affairs of man? Mounier answered these questions in the affirmative. He believed it to be his responsibility to make his faith relevant to his times. Mounier's Personalism constituted his effort to meet this responsibility. Personalism was a philosophy and ethics for our times.

The questions which Mounier confronted belong to every Christian who believes humanity to be a matter of his responsibility. Some of these questions are among the most traditional Christian questions; they ask of the Christian's right to intervene in politics, to show allegiance to civil authorities by holding office or serving in the military forces. Others ask of a Christian's responsibility to help secure social justice, to engage in revolution, and to collaborate with non-believers in political activity. All these questions, which reach the very center of a Christian's reflections, forever invite one to distinguish between the heavenly and the earthly, the material and the spiritual, the things of Christ and Caesar. None of these distinctions are easily made.

In 1932, the young Mounier began the journal *Esprit*. It became the central activity of his life and his primary vehicle to speak to his times. *Esprit's* founding issue carried a lead article titled "To Remake the Renaissance." There Mounier argued that five centuries of Western Civilization were coming undone. A new civilization had to be founded.

Mounier identified the civilization in crisis as bourgeois civilization. The bourgeois, for Mounier, were that entire social class of selfish individuals. They were dead to everything of value: religion, art, and social justice. They were non-heroic, unfeeling, and self-satisfied. There wasn't a bone of poetry in them. The bourgeois also were depicted by Mounier as being the embodiment of the rational, individualistic secularism that destroyed community and attacked spirit.

Believer Mounier affirmed the critiques of the bourgeois advanced by Marx and Nietzsche. His critiques were both political and aesthetic. This meant, on the one hand, that Mounier shared with Marx the left critique of industrial-capitalism's destructive domination of society. On the other hand, in agreement with Nietzsche, Mounier judged the bourgeois to be the essence of anti-feeling, anti-heart, anti-life.[7]

Mounier's criticism of the bourgeois was the basis of his political position, which was "neither left nor right." Engaged in a purposeful symmetry (a kind of combative balancing common to the style of papal social encyclicals), Mounier supported left and right against the present order, and then attacked them equally as being an integral part of the present order.[8] He believed that the right was correct about the moral decadence and communal dissolution caused by the bourgeois liberal order. He supported the left's critique of the social injustice of the industrial capitalist order. Yet Mounier argued that both the left and right were the consequences as much as the analysts of the existing destructive order.

Mounier made individualism the commanding idea of bourgeois civilization and the principle of all alienation (be it religious, philosophical, or social). According to Mounier, individualism destroyed culture by separating ideas from truth, art from universals, and truth from politics. It negated the possibility of a human economy by establishing the dominance of the market, profit, and production at the expense of workers and society. It corrupted the public life by making self-interest, free-enterprise, and class concerns the measure of all human activity.

Assuming that liberalism was another expression of the metaphysical individualism which he had traced from the Renaissance on, Mounier argued that liberalism cut man off from all natural communities. Not entertaining the possibility that liberal individualism had done any good in the past, or that it carried within itself any spiritual impulses for the present, he judged liberalism to be anarchic, destructive, and anti-communitarian. He accused it of having created the modern egoist, that sovereign individual who is solitary, without ancestry or flesh, and endowed with an inefficacious freedom. Furthermore, he denounced liberalism for having sanctioned the most destructive social-economic forces: uncontrolled *laissez-faire* economics; abstract and contractual notions of government; and the primacy of law, money, and production.

According to Mounier, contemporary collectivisms were the direct result of liberalism. They were born out of their opposition to the destructive principles and processes of liberal individualism. Mounier conceived both individualism and collectivism as the two faces of bourgeois civilization.

Mounier believed that the present generation was witnessing a final struggle between individualism and collectivism. For Mounier, Fascism, National Socialism, and Communism were the most advanced expressions of collectivism. Each was an "inverted theocracy" that left no area of human activity outside its control.

In direct opposition to individualism and collectivism Mounier articulated his Personalism. The person and the community were made the opposite principles of the individual and the collective. Mounier absolutely rejected those individualistic definitions that make man's worth reside in his legal status, private thought and feeling, and those collective definitions that make the essence of man his race, class, and nation. The person for Mounier, though understood to be an irreducible unity, is defined as a mixture of spirit and body, thought and feeling, reflection and action. In no way is the person autonomous, separate from his material, social, and cultural conditions. The unique person is developed across a lifetime; the person is a consequence of will, decisions, and habits on the one hand, and the determinants of society and culture on the other.

For Mounier every person is of God. Sharing Augustine's idea,

Mounier believed that God is more intimate to the person than the person is to himself. That person is the central value of Personalism.

Mounier's concept of community followed from his idea of the person. The good community, in Mounier's opinion, provides the person with what is materially and spiritually necessary. Community supports the person's growth. Although Mounier drew equally from right and left in defining the ideals of the communities, family, education, and work, there is little doubt that Mounier's primary inspiration was the Church's social thought.⁹

Mounier's Personalism received its full form in the 1930s. It was not a systematic philosophy. It attempted to provide an ethics for this century. It offered a set of principles that criticized the present order and provided an ideal for the future. However, Mounier's Personalism was eclipsed by that rush of events which overran Europe at a dizzying pace from 1938 onward. Like all thought, Personalism seemed abstract in what H. S. Hughes has called "the decade of choice." As Europe increasingly moved towards war, events reduced ethics to being a matter of choices about nations and their armies.

Mounier and his collaborators at *Esprit* finally realized in 1938 that France's very survival was the first issue of the public good. Now they entered the world of action—not for the sake of realizing a Personalist civilization, but ironically to preserve "bourgeois, individualist France."

In the post-war Mounier did what events have frequently compelled twentieth century thinkers to do. He engaged in self-accusation. He judged himself guilty of trying to maintain a false purity. He and his pre-war *Esprit* collaborators had preferred a pure conscience to effective action. He also admitted that Personalism, however useful as a philosophy of values, was not in itself adequate to the tasks of offering a political philosophy and *praxis* (form of action) for the era. Also he made admissions that they should have been more open to alliances with the Marxists and the socialists in the pre-war period.

The Second World War taught Mounier yet other things.¹⁰ He now understood freedom, individualism, and republican institutions to be fundamental conditions of a good civilization. The liberal traditions as embodied in France, England, and elsewhere in the West, were no longer to be judged as a mere expression of bourgeois individualism. As a result of his short association with an independent Vichy school, Uriage, Mounier learned that the conservative rhetoric of family, land, region, person, community, corporation and nation could serve the ideologies of reaction, even fascism and totalitarianism. This discovery, along with his determined hatred of the ruling bourgeois and of capitalism, led Mounier to make explicit the tie between Personalism and socialism.

Nevertheless what Mounier desired had no precise political equivalent. Mounier wanted a revolution which was too radical to be realized in the confines of the Republic's political life. Neither the newly created Christian Democratic Party nor the revitalized Socialist Party of Léon Blum held any attraction for him. He considered them to be trapped within the premises and the practices of the bourgeois world. The Radicals were summarily dismissed by Mounier as fragments of the Third Republic's archaeology, and Mounier could not help but see De Gaulle as a fascist leader *malgré lui-meme*. Thus, aside from making one brief, abortive effort, along with Sartre and other left-wing French intellectuals, to form an independent radical party in 1947, Mounier continued to conduct his struggle for a new world outside the political arena.

One major part of Mounier's combat was for a France and a Europe freed from both American and Soviet domination. He specifically feared that all Europe would be transformed into a fortress to defend capitalism, leaving Europe's sole meaning a sterile, retrograde anti-Communism. He feared what he saw prefigured in the Marshall Plan and the Atlantic Pact: the inevitable preparation for *a war that no cause could justify, no civilization sustain.*

The idealized revolution that Mounier once declared essential for France and Western Europe now had to be fought for on a truly global scale. Mounier added to Charles Péguy's phrase "the revolution will be moral if it will be at all," the phrase "the revolution also will be social, if it will be at all." Mounier defined the revolution in terms of the worker and the city. This intensified Mounier's long-standing discussion with Marxism. Marxism appealed to Mounier for several reasons: Like no other doctrine, Marxism spoke out against the exploiter on behalf of the exploited. It had won the workers to its side. Its followers had filled the ranks of the Resistance. In Mounier's opinion, Marxism, like no other doctrine, had a claim not only to the legacy of 1789, but to the possibility of a second French Revolution. It seemed to Mounier (as it did to much of the French Left), capable of describing the present conditions of man while calling man to a better future. While critical of Marxism's philosophical assumption and the French Communist Party's subservience to Moscow, Mounier nevertheless believed that within the Communist Party there was a real revolutionary potential. In fact, Mounier's socialism grew out of his attempt to integrate Marxism and Personalism.

However, Mounier's path towards humanistic socialism did not lead beyond the horizons of his 1932 *Esprit* platform. For Mounier, the world was still in crisis. The diseases of individualism and collectivism prevailed. Christian leadership still was dominated by those middle class Christians who served neither humanity nor God. Nietzsche's attack against their mediocrity was still a favorite plaint of Mounier.

Mounier's response to the crisis also remained essentially the same as that of 1932. Without power, other than influence over a small circle of educated consciences, Mounier chose to bear witness to his age. He would take unto himself the era's agonies and possibilities. This he did until his death in 1950.

For Mounier, commitment was required, even though action promised no path to success. Mounier's ultimate reasons for commitment were not humanistic but Christian. His faith required him in conscience to continue the work of the Creation, the Incarnation, and the Redemption.

Yet the whole issue of political engagement, like Mounier's whole life, raises a host of issues. What does commitment mean? To what, and on what grounds, should one be committed? Are there commitments to humanity and its future that are other than political? And what commitments betray faith, church and God?

For thinkers without such a faith as Mounier's, commitment, as we now go on to see, is no less perplexing. Reasons to serve humanity are not easily found in this cruel era when states, revolutions, and war are the most powerful agencies of change.

NOTES

1. For the source of this chapter, see Joseph Amato, *Mounier and Maritain: A French Catholic Understanding of the Modern World* (University, Alabama, 1975), esp. 105-163.

2. For two general guides to twentieth century history, see H. S. Hughes' *Contemporary Europe* (Englewood Cliffs, New Jersey, 1965) and Hajo Holborn's *The Political Collapse of Europe* (New York, 1951). For three works, constituting separate volumes in the Langer series of the modern world, see Oron Hale's *The Great Illusion, 1900-1914* (New York, 1971), Raymond Sontag's *A Broken World, 1919-1939* (New York, 1971), and Gordon Wright's *The Ordeal of Total War, 1939-1945* (New York, 1968).

3. Pierre Renouvin, *Histoire des rélations internationales,* Vol. VIII, Part II: *Les crises du XXe siècle de 1929 à 1945* (Paris, 1958), 11, 15-16.

4. For three standard introductions to European intellectual life, see Rolland Stromberg's *European Intellectual History Since 1789* (New York, 1975), George

Mosse's *The Culture of Western Europe* (New York, 1961), and H. S. Hughes' *Consciousness and Society* (New York, 1961).

5. For two useful guides to France in the twentieth century, see David Thomson's *Democracy in France Since 1870* (New York, 1964) and Gordon Wright's *France in Modern Times: 1760 to the Present* (Chicago, 1960).

6. For four guides to Roman Catholicism in the twentieth century, see E. E. Hales' *The Catholic Church in the Modern World* (Garden City, New York, 1960), Carlo Falconi's *The Popes in the Twentieth Century* (Boston, 1967), Joseph Moody's *Church and Society: Catholic Social and Political Thought and Movement, 1789-1950* (New York, 1950), and Luigi Sturzo's *Church and State* (Notre Dame, 1962). For introductions to Catholicism in twentieth Century France, see William Rauch's "From Sillon to the Movement Republicain Populaire," *The Catholic Historical Review*, LVIII, No. 1 (April, 1972), 25-66, and William Bosworth's *Catholicism and Crisis in Modern France* (Princeton, 1962).

7. For general introductions to the climate of ideas Mounier shared, see Roy Pierce's *Contemporary French Political Thought* (New York, 1966), H. S. Hughes' *The Obstructed Path* (New York, 1968), David Caute's *Communism and the French Intellectuals, 1914-1960* (New York, 1964), and Victor Brombert's *The Intellectual Hero: Studies in the French Novel, 1880-1955* (Philadelphia, 1961).

8. Mounier's criticisms of the bourgeois are voiced throughout all his major writings. Of particular use for this criticism and the articulation of his Personalism is *A Personalist Manifesto* (New York, 1938) and *Personalism* (Notre Dame, 1970).

9. For social encyclicals of the popes of the last two centuries, see Anne Freemantle, ed., *The Papal Encyclicals in Their Historical Context* (New York, 1956).

10. For three works useful for understanding intellectual climate, see Roland Stromberg's *After Everything, Western History Since 1945* (New York, 1975), Mario Einaudi and François Goguel's *Christian Democracy in Italy and France* (Notre Dame, 1952), and Michel-Antoine Burnier's *Choice of Action: The French Intellectuals on the Political Front Line* (New York, 1968).

CHAPTER SEVEN

Albert Camus and Jean-Paul Sartre: Humanists in an Inhuman Era

TWENTIETH CENTURY REALITY denied eighteenth and nineteenth century optimistic hopes. Total war, social anarchy, economic disorder, and totalitarianism suggested that twentieth century humanity was not its own savior but its own destroyer. Internationalism, the League of Nations, constitutional democracy, liberalism, and socialism, as well as other institutions which embodied those noble hopes, paled before new dark, violent forces.

Mounier's Personalism was an attempt to establish a philosophy for our era. He confronted the agonizing events of his time with the attitude of "tragic optimism," which held that God's love assured men and women that their existence need not be in vain, however tragic the outcome of their lives and history. In contrast, secular humanists had no such grounds for optimism. They had to bear the collective tragedies of this century without transcendent faith. The most positive attitude they could summon to themselves was at most a kind of courageous pessimism, which argued: persist even though progress is no longer certain, though there is no assurance that we can avoid self-extermination.

Humanism became a torturous matter in this century. The value of man was no longer certain. Two twentieth century French thinkers who reveal the crisis in contemporary humanism are Albert Camus and Jean-Paul Sartre.[1] Camus and Sartre raise fundamental ethical questions, such as: On what grounds do we believe in humanity? Is humanity merely a concept, perhaps even an abstraction, which should not weigh in our values? How do we serve humanity and the future of humanity in an era when states and revolutions become more violent and absolute? How can one be a humanist in our era? Or, last, should we turn away from the public world for the sake of the private world of self, family, and friend?

ALBERT CAMUS, A HUMANIST'S RESISTANCE

At the start of their careers, both Camus and Sartre were ambitious writers. Words were their profession. The outbreak of the Second World War interrupted what can be considered their artistic cultivation of private despair. The necessity of choice occupied them thereafter.

Neither brought to that commitment a real faith in progress. They believed that every cause could be an object of bad faith, and betrayal. They both were attracted to the pessimistic formula that man was condemned to act in a hopeless world.

Camus' work testified to that pessimism. Nurtured in the deep psychological tradition of Dostoevsky, Nietzsche, and others, Camus' paradoxical goal was to find a meaningful way to exist in a meaningless world. The characteristic concept of his work is "the absurd." The absurd, for Camus, is found in the human condition of suffering needlessly, without consolation; suffering even the absence of a reason for living.

In a series of essays titled *The Myth of Sisyphus* (1941), Camus juxtaposed the inherent human need for reason and happiness against the realities of an irrational and painful world. The absurd "is born of the confrontation between the human need and the unreasonable silence of the world." "The absurd is sin without God." Against the absurd world, Camus praised the rebellions of Dostoevsky's condemned creatures. With no amount of youthful bravado, he suggested the world's absurdity. Play acting, multiple loves, and revolt are tributes to the human attempts to preserve dignity in a world whose absurdity defeats in advance any of these efforts.

Camus, however, ended these essays, not on the moutain top with praise of the proud rebel, Prometheus, but in the shadowy depths of Hades, with praise of Sisyphus. He transformed Sisyphus' plight (being eternally condemned to the futile task of rolling too heavy a boulder up too steep a slope) into an ennobling act of defiance; his resistance to his very fate, his heroism and his ethics.

> I leave Sisyphus at the foot of the mountain! One always finds one's burden again. But Sisyphus teaches the higher fidelity that negates the gods and raises rocks. He too, concludes that all is well. This universe henceforth, without a master, seems to him neither sterile nor futile. Each atom of that stone, each mineral flake of that nightfilled mountain, in itself forms a world. The struggle itself

toward the heights is enough to fill a man's heart. One must imagine Sisyphus happy.²

The Second World War interrupted Camus' literary career. He gave himself unreservedly to the Resistance. A new question appeared at the center of his work. He now asked *how can men act together for the good in a world infested by evil?* This moral situation was the essence of his novel, *The Plague* (1946): "The Plague (World War) had swallowed up everyone and everything. There are no longer individual destinies: only a collective destiny made of the plague and the emotions shared by all."³

In *Notebooks, 1935-1942*, Camus described the moral imperatives which must guide one's actions:

> It is always useless to try to cut oneself off, even from other people's stupidity. You can say: "I don't know about it." One either fights or collaborates. There is nothing less excusable than war and the appeal to nationalities. But once the war has come, it is cowardly to stand on one side under the pretext that one is not responsible. Ivory towers are down. Indulgence is forbidden for oneself as well as other people.⁴

In the post-war, Camus, like Mounier, was left without a form of politics to match his proclaimed ideal of commitment.⁵ Regarding the trials of French collaborators, he took the middle position, neither victim nor executioner—"*ni victime, ni bourreau.*" He unequivocally rejected capital punishment, specifically denounced evils of colonialism as well as injustices committed by capitalist and socialist regimes alike. He stayed on middle ground during an epoch when choices between capitalism and communism, colonialism and non-colonialism, were demanded. His unwillingness to give an absolute answer, however, did not translate into any sympathy for the work-a-day politics of the Fourth French Republic.

It was not Camus' predilection for the private side of life (which he pursued with such depth in a work like *The Fall*, 1956) that accounted for his inability to chose sides.⁶ Instead, it was Camus' understanding of power itself. Camus, moralist that he was, understood four truths about contemporary politics. First, politics can mean accepting, even wanting, the death of one's adversary.⁷ Second, social change costs blood. "It requires bucketsful of blood and centuries of history to lead to an imperceptible modification in human condition. Such is the law.

For years heads fall like hail, terror reigns, Revolution is touted, and one ends up by substituting constitutional monarchy for legitimate monarchy."[8] Third was a central truth he explored in his essays and plays: men often become mass murderers for their causes. Repeatedly Camus suggested that those who cause the most blood to flow are the same ones who believe they have history on their side. In a play entitled "The Just Assassins," the revolutionists, reminiscent of Dostoevsky's *Possessed*, demand of themselves the most insane commitments to prove their authenticity. For the most perfect community tomorrow they must commit the most horrid crime today: they must stand ready to shed the blood of even an innocent child. "Not until the day comes when we stop sentimentalizing about children," one character says, "will the revolution triumph, and we be the masters of the world."[9] The "logic" of this perspective can lead to the conclusion that conscience can be antirevolutionary, therefore immoral.

The fourth truth Camus understood is one which, though so often ignored, is yet made obvious by twentieth century experience: Men, with dangerous ideas, become disastrous for mankind when they gain the power of the state. From them comes what Camus has described as "a socialism of the gallows":

> States laden with too many crimes are getting ready to drown their guilt in even greater massacres. One kills for a nation or a class that has been granted divine status. One kills for a future society that has likewise been given divine status. Whoever thinks he has omniscience imagines he has omnipotence. Temporal idols demanding an absolute faith tirelessly decree absolute punishments. And religion devoid of transcendence kills great numbers of condemned men devoid of hope.[10]

In *The Rebel* (1951) Camus called the spiritual criminals of the last two centuries "metaphysical revolutionists." Their revolt was not aimed against specific forms of oppression, instead they were motivated by the desire to change reality itself. Confounding the immanent with the transcendent, they proposed earthly substitutes for God. (Sade did this with sexual perversity; Lautréamont with art; Nietzsche with will; Rousseau with society; Hegel with history; Marx with the future.) Cruelest of these new gods, Camus argued, have been "the gods of history." The present becomes, as Hegel defined it, the perpetual struggle to dominate the forces which make tomorrow. "The entire history of mankind is, in any case, nothing but a prolonged fight of death for the conquest of universal prestige and absolute power."[11]

Camus, ally of Sisyphus, harshly judged the left's favorite god, Prometheus, who was "the tragic mask of twentieth century power":

> Proclaiming his hatred of the gods and his love of mankind, he turns away from Zeus with scorn and approaches mortal men in order to lead them in an assault against the heavens. But men are weak and cowardly; they must be organized. . . . Thus Prometheus, in his turn, becomes a master who first teaches and then commands. Men doubt that they can safely attack the city of light and are even uncertain whether the city exists. They must be saved from themselves. The hero then tells them that he, and he alone, knows the city . . . Prometheus alone has become god and reigns over the solitude of men. But from Zeus he has gained only solitude and cruelty; he is no longer Prometheus, he is Caesar.[12]

Camus' judgment of Prometheus was joined to his judgment of the revolutionists and the state they seek to win:

> All modern revolutions have ended in a reinforcement of the power of the State. 1789 brings Napoleon; 1848, Napoleon III; 1917, Stalin; the Italian disturbances of the twenties, Mussolini; the Weimar Republic, Hitler. . . . Apart from the few explanations that are not the subject of this essay, the strange and terrifying growth of the modern State can be considered as the logical conclusion of inordinate technical and philosophical ambitions, foreign to the true spirit of rebellion, but which nevertheless have given birth to the revolutionary spirit of our time. The prophetic dream of Marx and the over-inspired predictions of Hegel or of Nietzsche ended by conjuring up, after the city of God had been razed to the ground, a rational or irrational State, which in both cases, however, was founded on terror.[13]

The conservative implications of Camus' argument could not be ignored. He had indicted the revolutionary left. He chose to defend, rather than to remake man. Camus wanted no new man. Camus believed too much in human bodies—took too much pleasure from the ambiance of his native Algiers—to make them abstractions. Camus would not sacrifice the sensual and the intimate to ideology. Today's concrete existence must be defended against the abstract, idealized dreams of tomorrow. Ethics, for Camus, had its purpose in the defense of and the limits of humanity.

Jean-Paul Sartre understood Camus' position, and judged Camus harshly for it. In the course of a debate which sprang up as a consequence of Sartre's journal *Les temps moderns*' critical review of *The Rebel*, Sartre charged Camus with having abandoned history, and leaving man a helpless victim before the forces which encompass him.[14] Camus, Sartre said, who once told man "to expect nothing from heaven", now asks him to expect nothing from himself or his future. Camus, Sartre further contended, placed man's dignity in a form of revolt which was a mere futile, psychological exercise. Sartre argued that Camus had judged man guilty in advance for taking any action that could improve his condition.

JEAN-PAUL SARTRE, ETHICAL EXPERIMENTS IN SELF-DEFINITION[15]

Jean-Paul Sartre, more than any other, is the embodiment of a contemporary intellectual of the left.[16] Until the Second World War, Sartre's preoccupation was literature and philosophy. (His existentialism, in large measure, was a result of the marriage he effected between the depth philosophies of Heidegger and Husserl and nineteenth and twentieth century introspective literature.) With the war, Sartre was compelled by what he called *"la force des choses,"* the power of things, to commit himself to the public world. The French Resistance Movement against the Nazis, as he experienced it and idealized it, was a founding ethical experience for Sartre.

Sartre's commitment since the war passed through several stages. First, in 1945, along with Merleau-Ponty, he founded the journal *Les temps moderns.*[17] It was predicated on the proposition that man is his history—his conditions, freedom and possibilities. It falls to man to save himself. History is a vast courtroom where the future is judged. In 1947 the desire to intervene directly into the politics of France led Sartre to found the party, *Rassemblement du Peuple Français.* Attracting only intellectuals, the party was short-lived and of no real consequence.

Second, as editor of *Les temps moderns* in the 1952 to 1956 period, Sartre increasingly lent his support directly to the Communist Party at home and abroad. His writings became more dependent on Marxism.

Reacting to the 1956 Soviet invasion of Hungary, Sartre entered a new stage. He resumed the role of being critic of the Soviet Union and the subservient French Communist Party. Sartre increasingly made his cause the peoples of the third world. In the late 1950s and the early 1960s, he took the side of the native Algerians against the French colonists. He supported Castro and the Cuban Revolution. As critic of American capitalism and world-wide imperialism he was in harmony with an emerging new left in the United States: Sartre supported the

Black Civil Rights movement in the United States and condemned American involvement in Vietnam. At the 1967 Lord Russell War Crimes Trial in Paris, Sartre took a leading role in prosecuting Americans for being guilty of genocide in Vietnam.[18]

Sartre gave his full support to the 1968 student uprising in France, *les événements de mai*. His support of the most radical students led him to a fourth and last stage of his political development.[19] He indicted his past vocation as simply a literary engagement, which allowed him conveniently to express his moralism without sacrificing his career and the benefits he derived from it. Sartre now put himself entirely at the service of France's militant Maoist youth.[20] He not only worked for them with a remarkable intensity (putting in nineteen hours a day), but even more, he consciously allowed his reputation to be exploited by them for their own ends.

Sartre's evolution not only contradicted that more common political path which leads aging intellectuals from left to right, but it anticipated the formation of the new American left: He argued that technology did not necessarily liberate, but that it could enslave man. Europe and the West were no longer at the center of history. The future of the revolutionary struggle lay with the non-White, colonial people. History itself offers no guarantees of victory.

Sartre's unity with the new left manifests itself in the type of victims who populate his work. Although one meets in Sartre's writings victims of economic exploitation and racial prejudice, the majority of his victims are the spiritually abused—the pariahs of society, whose ideas, sexuality, or crimes make them outcasts. Sartre, Molnar observed, is the ally of the bastard.[21] The outcast is his ethical ideal. His favorite hero-victims, the subject of separate biographical studies, are intellectuals such as Baudelaire, Nizan, and Genet.[22] They are all young men without fathers, secure families, or certain social definition. Sartre's fictive creations, as well as his biographical portraits, share a common alienation. They are without social presence. They live as students and artists often have. They are poor; like Dostoevsky's Raskolnikov, or so many other anti-heroes of modern depth literature, they occupy the small, dark spaces. They live along the sidewalks of impersonal cities. They look for relief from themselves. They sense themselves to be estranged, not belonging to anything or anyone. Commerce and politics are alien to them. As for respect, honor, and status, they want or have none. They have been given nothing; no tradition sustains them. They are, to use Sartre's language, "sequestered," walled off from social life. They have only their own thought. It must be used against themselves and others for what meaning they can gain. Ethics for them involves the struggle for self-definition.

These near-presentless, bodiless creatures of Sartre's creation are born of Sartre's philosophy of life. They reflect a world of uncertain reciprocities. Sartre's philosophy (particularly as formulated in his major treatise, *Being and Nothingness*) envisions man in existence as being absolutely alone and totally free of any governing order of ideas or nature; an existence which does not concede any binding human responsibilities. There is, in Sartre's view, only the free, solitary individual who must will his meaning against himself and others. In this Manichean view, betrayal is always possible. Within the individual there exists the ever-present temptation to betray one's freedom by identifying oneself entirely with one's condition or role in order to escape the responsibility of using one's freedom to define oneself. Sartre labeled that false objectivization of oneself – the defining of oneself as a thing (a being-in-itself) – "bad faith."

Outside himself the individual is engaged in a permanent war. He must constantly struggle against the others, who attempt to take possession of him by defining him simply as an object for their existence. "Everything which holds for me," Sartre wrote, arguing an aggressive individualism, "holds for him. While I attempt to free myself from the hold of the Other, the Other is trying to free himself from mine; while I seek to enslave the Other, the Other seeks to enslave me."[23] The very look itself of the Other ignites self-consciousness with the threat of being turned into an object. The very look of the Other, and the shame it elicits, establishes the truth that "I am this self which another knows. And this self which I know – this I am in the world which the Other has made alien to me."[24]

Sartre envisioned no escape from these interior and exterior threats to the self. For inside there is in truth only freedom – and the senses of anguish, superfluousness, and gratuity which one's freedom nurtures. "In anguish," Sartre writes elsewhere, "I apprehend myself at once as totally free and as not being able to derive the meaning of the world except as coming from myself."[25]

To the man of such a consciousness there comes the anguish of knowing that he is the source of all values. Orestes, the afflicted protagonist of Sartre's *Flies*, said: "And there was nothing left in heaven, no Good, nor Evil, no one to command me."[26] "Man," Sartre wrote elsewhere, "is condemned to be free . . . to carry the weight of the whole world on his shoulders; he is responsible for the world and for himself as a way of being."[27]

Sartre carried this desperate individualism further when he wrote of this I, whose freedom establishes both value and nothingness in the world:

> Every human reality is a passion in that it projects losing itself so as to found being and at the same time to constitute the in-itself which escapes contingency by being its own foundation, the *ens causa sui*, which religions call God. Thus the passion of man is the reverse of that of Christ, for man loses himself as man in order that God may be born. But the idea of God is contradictory and we lose ourselves in vain. Man is a useless passion.[28]

As Sartre's literature mirrors his philosophy, so his philosophy is but an extension of his search for self. All Sartre's writing is ultimately autobiographical – or narcissistic, argued Victor Brombert:

> The fact is that Sartre, perhaps more than any other contemporary writer, is a victim of peculiar mirror-disease of thought. A special narcissism compels him to stare at his own image at the same time as he resents that confining and defining glance. Young Hugo, in *Les Mains Sales*, carries photographs of himself in his suitcase. They represent the burden of his past, as well as the eye of the self which allows the Sartrean intellectual hero no respite. Roquentin is thus trapped by himself, trapped by the mobile refractions of his own accusing eye. Intelligence, above all, is in the Sartrean terms a form of life imprisonment.[29]

The truth of Brombert's insight is confirmed by Sartre's *Words*, an autobiographical inquiry into the early years of his youth.[30] There we meet a lonely child, who was without a father. He was in love with his mother who, since the death of Sartre's father, has had to return to live with her parents. In her parents' household she too lived as if she were a child, and thus she was more like a sister than a mother to Sartre. Her father, Charles Schweitzer, was for Sartre the quintessence of the detestable, domineering, cultured, upper class bourgeois.

The young Sartre was the child who learned to live for the show he put on, "who respected adults on the condition they idolized me."[31] "Books," Sartre wrote of his secluded childhood, "were my birds and my nests, my household pets, and my countryside."[32] His first adventures were in libraries. His first, and ultimately last, ambition became to write: to make his words a gift to the world. And that gift would make him immortal. "I discovered that in belles lettres the Giver can be transformed into his own Gift, that is, into a pure object. Chance had made me a man, generosity would make me a book."[33] Sartre knew himself to be a pretense, and therefore, expected the rest of the world to be sham.

> Condemned to please, I endowed myself with charms that withered on the spot. Everywhere I went, I dragged about my false good nature, my idle importance on the alert for a new opportunity. When I thought that I had seized it, I would strike a pose only to find once again the hollowness which I was trying to get away from.... I was a fake child, I was holding a fake salad-washer. I could feel my acts changing into gestures. Play-acting robbed me of the world and of human beings. I saw only roles and props. Serving the activities of adults in a spirit of buffoonery, how could I have taken their worries seriously? I adapted myself to their intentions with a virtuous eagerness that kept me from sharing their purposes. A stranger to the needs, hopes, and pleasures of the species, I squandered myself coldly in order to charm it. It was my audience; I was separated from it by footlights that forced me into a proud exile which quickly turned to anguish.[34]

Of all the literary figures, Sartre wrote, he most resembled Baudelaire. Like Baudelaire, he had to attempt to construct meaning for his life despite the nearly overwhelming feeling that his existence was entirely gratuitous. As with Baudelaire, an unresolved Oedipal complex, profound solitude, and a desperate need for self-definition, all warred within him. Engaged in self-revelation, Sartre wrote of Baudelaire:

> People have taken every opportunity of attributing an unresolved Oedipus complex to him, but it matters little whether or not he desired his mother. I should rather say that he refused to resolve the theological complex which transforms parents into gods. He refused to resolve it because it was necessary in order to evade the law of solitude and find in other people a remedy against gratuitousness, to confer on other people, or rather on certain other people, a sacred character. What he wanted was neither friendship, love, nor relations on equal terms: He had no friends or at most a few intimates among the riff-raff. He wanted judges—beings whom he could deliberately place beyond the fundamental law on contingency, beings who existed simply because they had the right to exist and whose decrees conferred on him in his turn a stable and sacred 'nature.' He was ready to appear guilty in their eyes; and 'guilty in their eyes' meant absolutely guilty. But the guilty man has his function in the theocratic universe. He has his function and his rights. He

has a right to censure, to punishment, and to repentance. He cooperates with the universal order and his misdoing invests him with a religious dignity, a place apart in the hierarchy of beings.[35]

Sartre was of Rousseau's lineage. Ethics was an aspect of self-definition. Self-consciousness dominated his being. He sought his meaning in the writing of words. They would serve him as heart, family, life, as a kind of immortality: a psychological defense against the impermanence and impertinence of things. Like Rousseau, Sartre had to live with the sense of the infinity and the finitude of his self. Therefore he was his own curse and blessing.

Sartre knew all this about himself. And that awareness was his burden. It made him vividly experience how superfluous his life was, how vain his art. Alternatively, he was fascinated and nauseated by his own self-awareness. At times he mocked, despised, and hated himself for it, and therein lay the roots of his hatred for his own background, the bourgeois.

He repeated André Gide's spiteful dictum, *"Famille, je vous haïs!"* The slightest palpitations of his spirit were in succession his anguish and pleasure, his torment and pride, and always his most absorbing preoccupation.

The disgust and boredom caused by his narcissism drove Sartre to look to others for his meaning. And yet, he despised others for the meanings which they both gave him and denied him. At times he unreservedly cast all his moral support to the masses. They, he judged, were real, embodied, authentic in a way he, of the safe, secluded world, could not be. They were sincere; he, insincere. They were potent; he, impotent.

This brutal self-judgment frequently led Sartre, as it leads so many intellectuals, to prefer deed over word, action over thought, combat over philosophy. Thought itself seems somehow to be immoral. At times, as in his preface to Frantz Fanon's *Wretched of the Earth*, Sartre supported violent extremes. There he sympathetically reconstructed Fanon's argument: killing Whites was essential for Black psychological liberation.

Through a process of counter-identity—which always was formed in opposition to the bourgeois, capitalist West—Sartre sought to escape his own nihilistic self-circlings. He would serve the downtrodden. They gave him a public identity and an ethics. He would make their liberation his just cause. Thus, Sartre could escape his own subjectivity—and at times, feel himself to be regaining the high purposes of nineteenth century progressive humanism.

Sartre held that ground with difficulty. The self was always the temptation. The affairs of men in society were often, in his literature, only backdrops for his celebration of the solitary victim. Among Sartre's hero-victims are Orestes, the Resistance fighters, all those individuals who—not unlike Camus' Sisyphus—"by sheer force of will set limits to the torturers' power to negate his autonomy as a free man."[36] "All Sartrean 'free' men" are, in the words of Germaine Brée, "participants in a mystic sacrifice."[37]

To be pure, to be redeemed, simply to cure his own neurosis—all three of these ends run together in Sartre's thought—Sartre sacrificed himself for the sake of his writing. He would martyr himself for his words. He would willingly make himself "a martyr-comedian" of ideas. He would put all his "senseless picking" at himself in the service of mankind. By making his mind a kind of purgatory, he presumed to suffer spiritually what the rest of mankind suffered bodily. He would be what Baudelaire declared himself to be, ". . . the wound and the knife, the victim and the executioner."[38]

He would be a Romantic Socrates. To meet his responsibilities, Sartre would reach the bottom. Expressing an aggressive, masochistic narcissism, he wrote at the conclusion of *Words*:

> I took my pen for a sword; I now know we're powerless. No matter. I write and will keep writing books; they're needed; all the same, they do serve some purpose. Culture doesn't save anything or anyone, it doesn't justify. But it's a product of man: he projects himself into it, he recognizes himself in it; that critical mirror alone offers him his image. Moreover, that old, crumbling structure, my imposture, is also my character: one gets rid of a neurosis, one doesn't get cured of one's self. Though they are worn out, blurred, humiliated, thrust aside, ignored, all of the child's traits are still to be found in the quinquagenarian.[39]

Sartre is not all that different from Rousseau, who introduced his *Confessions* by calling all, if they dare, to stand openly in moral comparison with him. Nor is Sartre different from all those intellectuals who create by consciousness of self and by artifice of words. Sartre was his writing. For the sake of it he had emptied himself of memory, class, stature, and tradition. His books, as he knew so well, were his costumes. . . . And all of us moderns should ask: How different are we from Sartre?

INTELLECTUALS AND THE MYTH OF HUMANITY

Sartre is typical of the secular intellectuals who concluded that man is an historical creature. Thus he faced the terrifying recognition that man makes himself: he is his own savior or executioner. This vision set forth the guilt-laden proposition that man is his own god. His self-guiding providence is absolute, yet temporal.[40]

This spiritual condition of intellectuals like Sartre is described by Jean Guitton: "Around 1880, one could say: *Even the guilty are innocent.* In 1950, it is necessary to reverse the terms of that formula and say: *Even the innocent are guilty.*"[41] Like Sartre and Camus, the young European intellectuals of the following two generations continued to embrace the guilt-inducing assumption that man is responsible for man; that sin, if only by omission, consists of not realizing the highest dreams of the eighteenth, nineteenth, and twentieth centuries. Consequently, these intellectuals judge severely. They start with the premise that man has failed man; modern history is a story not of success but of failure.[42]

For a whole generation of intellectuals and to a degree, for the West itself, Sartre brought the eighteenth century humanist vision to its term: Man had become the measure. But what did the measure mean? What ethics came with this humanism? To answer these questions, other questions had to be answered first: Was man the measure of a glorified individual or an idealized collectivity? If man as individual or collectivity is the measure, what is it that joins men together across culture, ages, and existence itself?

Given what humanity has done and experienced in the twentieth century, some have come to believe that man as an ideal is dead. Man died with the progress he invented. Of this Michel Foucault has written: "Man was a recent invention and probably to go out of fashion shortly. From the death of God in the philosophy of the Enlightenment to the disappearance of Man (and of the Cartesian *cogito*) only two centuries had elapsed: time enough for the experiment of putting Man in God's place to have exposed its inherent dangers."[43]

If man is dead, then in whose name are we joined together? And without a myth to unify us can we have an ethics? And, finally, to ask the question that inspires our Conclusion, is ethics itself dead?

NOTES

1. For the lives and writings of Jean-Paul Sartre and Albert Camus, see the Bio-Bibliography.
2. Camus, *The Myth of Sisyphus and Other Essays* (New York, 1960), 21.
3. Camus, *The Plague* (New York, 1958), 151.
4. Camus, *Notebooks, 1935–1942* (New York, 1963), 143.

5. Useful for understanding Camus' positions in the post-war are his *Notebooks*, Vol. II (New York, 1966) and a collection of his essays on the liberation, Hungary, and Algeria, *Resistance, Rebellion, and Death* (New York, 1960).

6. In the tradition of French moralists from Montaigne and Pascal to Gide and Bernanos, Camus' first interests were private instead of public. As Germaine Brée wrote, "Camus deplored the almost total politicization of life. It, too, was a form of plague," *Camus and Sartre* (New York, 1972) 203. Camus' preferences were for the aesthetic instead of the political. The *Fall*, for example, resembles Dostoevsky's *Notes From the Underground*. It takes the form of the confession of a sick soul. The protagonist explains how once he lived only to shine in the eyes of others, how above all else he preferred an image of being a generous man. However, his failure to respond to the cries of a drowning woman is a knife in his heart. Inside he is judged to be guilty. "Men," he says, "are never convinced of your reasons, your sincerity, of the seriousness of your suffering, except by your death. So long as you are alive, your case is doubtful; you have a right only to their skepticism," 74. His life is consumed by his attempt to elude the judgments of others. He, of course, fails. And in the end he reaches the most horrifying position of all: He elects to find his innocence by joining all men who are *innocent* by virtue of their collective consciencelessness. It is fascination for themes like those of the *Fall* that dominated the interests of Camus.

7. Camus, *Notebooks, 1942–1951* (New York, 1965), 119.

8. *Ibid.*

9. Camus, *Just Assassins, Caligula and Three Other Plays* (New York, 1966), 256.

10. Camus, "Reflections on the Guillotine," *Resistance, Rebellion and Death* (New York, 1960), 228.

11. Camus, *The Rebel, An Essay on Man in Revolt* (New York, 1956), 139.

12. *Ibid.*, 244–245.

13. *Ibid.*, 177.

14. Sartre's "Reply to Camus" from *Les temps moderns* is available in *Situations* (Greenwich, Conn., 1965), 54–81. Two useful discussions of this debate are found in Burnier's *Choice of Action* and Brée's *Camus and Sartre*, esp. 1–14.

15. For a useful bibliographic guide to Sartre, see *Yale French Studies*, XXX (1963), 108–119 and Benjamin Suhl's *Jean-Paul Sartre* (New York, 1970), 273–286. Helpful introductory studies to Sartre are Philip Thody's *Sartre. A Biographical Introduction* (New York, 1971), ed. Edith Kern's *Sartre. A Collection of Critical Essays* (Englewood Cliffs, N.J., 1962), R. D. Laing and D. G. Coopers' *Reason and Violence. A Decade of Sartre's Philosophy, 1950–1960* (New York, 1971), and ed. Mary Warnock's *Sartre. A Collection of Critical Essays* (Garden City, N.Y., 1971). Two works, of different inspiration, but both highly critical of Sartre, are Raymond Aron's *History of the Dialectic of Violence, An Analysis of Sartre's Critique de la Raison Dialectique* (New York, 1975) and Thomas Molnar's *Sartre: Ideologue of Our Time* (New York, 1968).

16. For an understanding of the development of Sartre's thought and his growing tie to the left, see the autobiographical works of his life-long compan-

ion, Simone Beauvoir *The Prime of Life* (New York, 1962) and *Force of Circumstances* (New York, 1965); Stanley Hoffman's "The Paradoxes of the French Political Community," *In Search of France* (New York, 1963), 1-117; H. S. Hughes, *The Obstructed Path. French Social Thought in the Years of Desperation, 1930-1960* (New York, 1968), esp. 153-226; George Lichtheim, *Marxism in Modern France* (New York, 1966); Raymond Aron, *The Opium of the Intellectuals* (New York, 1962); and Mark Poster, *Existential Marxism in Postwar France* (Princeton, N.J., 1975).

17. For Sartre's relation to Merleau-Ponty, see Sartre's "Merleau-Ponty," *Situations*, 156-226. For Ponty's shared philosophy of a historical commitment which led to justification of the Communist Party, see Maurice Merleau-Ponty's *Humanism and Terror* (Boston, 1969, orig. Fr. Edit., 1947). Useful to understand the general transformation of European thought from idealism to existentialism and historicism, see George Lichtheim, *Europe in the Twentieth Century* (New York, 1972), 211-239.

18. For examples of pieces reflecting Sartre's commitment to causes, see *Sartre on Cuba* (New York, 1961); "Vietnam: Imperialism and Genocide," "Czechoslovakia; The Socialism that Came in from the Cold," "France: Masses, Spontaneity, Party," *Between Existentialism and Marxism*, 67-137; *On Genocide* (Boston, 1968), and Sartre's preface to Frantz Fanon's *The Wretched of the Earth* (New York, 1968), 7-31.

19. See for Sartre of *Les Événements de Mai*, 1968, an interview "Itinerary of a Thought," *New Left Review*, no. 58 (Nov.-Dec., 1969), 43-66, and *Les communistes ont peur de la revolution* (Paris, 1967).

20. For Sartre's support of Maoism and the radical youth, see his interviews in *New York Review of Books* (March 26, 1970), *Esquire* (Dec., 1972), and *L'Espresso* (Feb., 11, 1973).

21. Molnar, *Sartre*, 47.

22. *Baudelaire* (Paris, 1947), *Saint-Genet, comédien et martyr* (Paris, 1952), and his preface to Nizan's *Aden arabie* (Paris, 1961), 9-62.

23. From *Being and Nothingness*, excerpted in *The Philosophy of Jean-Paul Sartre*, ed. Robert Cumming (New York, 1965), 209.

24. Ibid., 199.

25. Ibid., 129.

26. Sartre, *Flies*, ibid., 240.

27. Excerpted from *Being and Nothingness*, ibid., 277.

28. Ibid., 352.

29. Victor Brombert, "Jean-Paul Sartre, Techniques and 'Impossible' Situations," *Modern Language Quarterly* vol. 30 (Summer, 1969), 442.

30. *The Words* (Greenwich, Conn., 1964).

31. Ibid., 20.

32. Ibid., 30.

33. Ibid., 121.

34. Ibid., 53.

35. Sartre, *Baudelaire* (New York, 1950), 55-56.

36. Brée, *Camus and Sartre*, 161.

37. *Ibid.*, 161-162.
38. Sartre, *Baudelaire*, 26.
39. *The Words*, 159.
40. For a discussion of how the terror of man's historicity affected the high culture of post-World War Two Europe, see Lichtheim's *Europe*, 358-372.
41. Cited in Jean Lacroix's *Les sentiments et la vie morale* (Paris, 1952), 23. Emphasis mine.
42. The historiographical theme of surveying history as a failure is brilliantly explored by A. W. Salomone, "The Risorgimento between Ideology and History: The Political Myth of Rivoluzione Mancata," *American Historical Review*, LXVIII (Oct., 1962), 38-56.
43. This is Lichtheim's paraphrase of Michel Foucault, *Europe*, 370.

CONCLUSION

Is Ethics Dead?

THE INDIVIDUAL MAY BE the unique creation of modernity. In the modern world, everything about the individual—his rights, opinions, feelings, career, and potential—have all been reasons to alter economics, to issue new bills of rights, and to overturn societies. In the modern world it is no longer assumed that the individual should be sacrificed to the good of the family, traditional values, or to social interests. In his privacy, property, and intimacy, the individual has triumphed.

Modern ethical theories, from Rousseau and Marx to Mounier and Camus, testify to the ascent of the individual. Egoisms of all sorts register ethically the individual's full scale emergence in modern history. The American Revolution and the French Revolution were universal manifestoes for individual rights. The cult of the unique person was born out of Romanticism. (We noted this cult in the works of Rousseau, Dostoevsky, Nietzsche, and Sartre.) In this century, life-plan conceptions of ethics (revealing the confidence and prosperity of many) conceive of values in relation to the full development of one's life. And though far more pessimistic, existentialisms also attribute first importance to the individual. It argues that the individual's essence consists of his choices.

Rousseau, it would seem, has won out. The cult of the self is now a universal religion. Individualism, as prescriptive or descriptive, is made the central organizing principle of our world. The phenomenal growth of psychology in the modern literate West in this century is the strongest proof of this. Every aspect of the individual is considered to be worthy of interest. Psychology is not alone in its interest in the self. Looking at ourselves has become a major cultural enterprise; for many, it is their most important activity.

The victory of individualism, as Marx and Mounier testify, has not been welcomed by all. From different points of view, individualism has been judged to be against God, man, and society. Contemporary critics Richard Sennett and Christopher Lasch have argued that the victory of the individual has been at the expense of the public life. Our consuming interest in self has equaled, according to them, a waning interest in community; our obsessive preoccupation with the self replaces participation in politics.[1] They say we suffer "the tyranny of intimacy." In place of justice we have put social therapy. The therapeutic ethic has come, in their judgment, to occupy in our times the place which the utilitarian ethic held in the preceding century.

The triumph of the individual, it can be argued, means that ethics is dead. For ethics to exist reason and freedom must exist in community. We must be joined in beliefs about the good, not simply be part of a disciplined collective order. If we value nothing sufficiently to embody it in a community, there is, in fact, no ethics at all.

Even if we do not entirely accept the proposition that ethics depends upon the existence of an ethical community, we should not adopt the opposite contention that only the individual is moral.[2] This conception denies the social nature of man. Individualism is formed by a culture, not given by nature. Although we may not be a herd animal, without community our ethical compass is set spinning.

Today confusion is the situation of most of us. We belong to a variety of local, regional, ethnic, traditional, and religious communities, but they are not of adequate strength to value and to order our changing world. We are surrounded by a host of differing cultures—by popular, traditional, secular, and religious, as well as ethnic, national, legal, class, mass, and elite—but no single one of them commands. Furthermore the public world, which informs us about arguments for and against nearly everything, makes all things a matter of dispute.

This conflict of cultures and public life enters into us, and fills us with contradiction. And in this uncertain condition, we are left unsure as to how to nurture our children, to grow old, to suffer, even to die. Specialists spring up everywhere. They claim to instruct us about how to deliver our children, to make love, to be assertive, to mourn, even to be sane. It seems nothing is inherited. Nothing is clearly right or wrong. There can be no ethics where there are neither shared assumptions nor common language.

The conflict of cultures and the division of contemporary communities make us aware how much our world is dominated by economic, social, technological and political collectivities. They shape our existences more than anything else. In fact, we recognize that our very ability to embody value publicly depends upon our ability to control these collectivities. Not to control them is to admit that we are powerless in the world. And this admission is tantamount to saying that we are not ethically responsible for our own creation.

Our ability to control the collectivities raises the question whether we can control our own government. Or rather shall we ask whether we can make the state an agency of our freedom? Or is the state another vast collectivity that determines us? This question presses particularly on us Americans, who have long presumed to have the right and the power to create a better world for mankind. If we despair of the state's ability to build a better world, have we not despaired of a better future for mankind?

Here we reach the question of the relationship between our ethics and our citizenship. For a significant number of Americans, citizenship and ethics reached a radical disjuncture during the Vietnam War.[3] Citizenship is the fundamental way we participate in the world at large. Our credo as Americans has long been that our government represents not only us but mankind. And it is this belief which leads us to an array of bewildering ethical contradictions.

No subject tests as war does. At issue here is our willingness to fight not only a war, but a nuclear war. Does our very citizenship involve us, if only tacitly, in the destruction of humanity? There are patriots who argue that for the sake of our nation and the great values it embodies, we must be willing to risk the destruction of humanity.[4] Conceding that sacrifice is essential to give value, we still must ask: What measure of sacrifice does our patriotism require?

Nuclear war challenges all sense of justice and fair exchange. Fair exchange, or mutual giving underlies human institutions, thought, and action.[5] The fundamental, the first and oldest, exchange between man and government (expressed so clearly by feudalism) is the trade of obedience for security.[6] Upon this basis, we ask, how do we enter into reciprocity with a state that threatens to destroy us and everything else. And we further ask, even if we choose to make such an exchange for ourselves, on what grounds do we make it for others. If, in fact, one child chooses to live instead of die, how do we justify our willingness to risk his existence?

The best argument to be made for preparation for nuclear war is a practical argument: we must risk total war in order to avoid total war. The threat, it is argued, gives integrity to our intentions. It leaves no misunderstanding about our seriousness. However this argument is judged, as compelling or insane, it is not in either case an ethical argument. It is a practical argument.

In fact, most political arguments are not ethical arguments. The state's arguments are almost always practical arguments. The state must choose, above all else, to be effective.

At the heart of all governments, I believe, exists the principles of *raison d'état.*[7] The state's ultimate goals are always the maintenance and the extension of its own power. No human interest can command the state to sacrifice itself. It honors only a superior force. (This does not deny the contention that the state can become the captive of classes and ideologies that might lead it to destruction by war or revolution.)

Jacques Ellul has argued that politics represents the commanding illusion of the contemporary world.[8] We continue to believe that we can realize what we desire through the political process. We falsely assume that the state, the parties and the bureaucracies which form it, are neutral. Do the state and its apparatus have interests of their own? Ellul writes:

> Political considerations permit us to think that we have the "general solution" because they permit us to do away at one stroke with all human reality and the search for truth. . . . The motives, the processes, the mysteries that made man accept religion and expect God to accomplish what he was unable to do, lead him nowadays into politics and make him expect those things from the state.[9]

Ellul's pessimism, though boldly formulated, is not unique to our century. On various grounds, with the use of differing literary forms (which range from social scientific analysis to anti-utopian literature), Western thinkers have abandoned faith in man's capacity to transform the world. No doubt, war, revolution, depression, and totalitarianism have provided Dostoevsky, Nietzsche, Adams, and other pessimists with great numbers of attentive students in this century. The inability of the developed nations to establish a justice, the near total destruction of archaic peoples, have fed the most extreme pessimisms.[10] Claude Levi-Strauss revealingly wrote in conclusion to his *The Origin of Table Manners:*

> In the present century, when man is actively destroying countless living forms, after wiping out so many societies whose wealth and diversity had, from time immemorial, constituted the better part of his inheritance, it has probably never been more necessary to proclaim, as do the myths, that sound humanism does not begin with oneself, but puts the world before life, life before man and respect for others before self-interest: and that no species, not even our own, can take the fact of having been on this earth for one or two million years—since, in any case, man's stay here will one day come to an end—as an excuse for appropriating the world as if it were a thing and behaving on it with neither decency nor discretion.[11]

Dark visions abide. In measure we all share them. We have created what we can't control. Our mindless technological, economic, and political creations fashion us as they will. We have cut ourselves off from God, nature, and tradition, and in doing this, we failed to discover freedom, but put ourselves in a field of relentless change. We lack a star to guide us. And unless we share a common light, what community is there? Are we not condemned to carry out our life's passage, separately, privately, without festival and ritual? Without shared myths, how do we celebrate and commemorate?

None of us surrenders entirely to pessimism. Our minds never altogether exclude the ideal of improvement. If only by the context to which we are joined, we are too modern to renounce the ideal of a better life. Whole schools of thought, parties, and newly-born nations value themselves with reference to the future they claim to serve. Unknowingly, even despite ourselves, we lend our allegiances, energies, actions, and hopes to progressive dreams. The first principle of the ethics of progress, our universal responsibility for human potentiality, still moves us.

In fact, we live between ferocious pessimisms and naive optimisms. The reasons for our middle position abound, and with these reasons comes a sense of being ethically stymied in our times. How do we know whether our actions will have good consequences? On what ground do we assume that our actions matter? These questions eat at us, as they did Sartre, Camus, and Mounier. They challenge our very inner sense of being ethical agents.

What confidence can we muster to counteract the deepening pessimism taught by daily affairs? Upon us seems to press the whole world—with all its needs and its immense injustice. Its screams are too many, too contradictory, too terrible to listen to. We know for sure there is a lot of pain in the world. And we do not want its grief. Neither our heart nor our reason is sufficient to encompass the whole world.

The world for us moderns never goes away. We cannot escape it. In the world we eat, work, get good deals and bad deals, and try to give ourselves a meaning. With it we have a host of different exchanges. We must forever judge and value the world. There is no choice.

Yet we know we are divided on fundamentals. We are not unified in our allegiances. Our loyalties are not certain: self, friends, family, work, church, private and public associations, all have their say within us. Clearly ethics is dead if it is supposed to resolve these disorders of allegiance and thought.

This suggestion that ethics is dead has a strange ring. Perhaps we deny ethics by asking too much of it. Ethics has an abiding place in human affairs, but its place is neither as dramatic nor as universal as thinkers such as Dostoevsky, Nietzsche, Adams, or Sartre believed. Afterall, ethics—as systematic reflection—has always had only a limited appeal. The great majority of us only think what we have learned to think. Even when we are confronted by bold contradictions, most often we do not choose ethics as a way to respond. Values are most often taken to be implicit in our living, not explicit guides for it.

We think ethically most often only when we cannot escape making a major decision—or when our culture dictates a discussion before certain types of situations. We suspect any argument which would judge ethics to be dead because we lack universal assumptions.

The history of ethical systems in particular, as well as of cultures in general, discloses a plurality of ideals. There is little reason to believe that what has essentially been true of human cultural diversity in the past will not be true in the future. The reasons for the plurality of human values are many. The human heart itself is always mixed. Its senses of happiness are not the same. Its notions of duty are in conflict. Its short-run pleasures and its long-run advantages invariably clash. And, despite our assumption of self-knowledge, in truth we do not know ourselves. To cite Pascal, "The heart has reasons which the mind does not know." Psychoanalysis suggests how radically we are divided between our basic instincts and society's rules of morality. We human beings have, as Dostoevsky knew so well, the bodies of animals and the minds of angels. Our pluralism defies, makes banal, those truisms about happiness, loyalty, duty, and the common good.

Human needs create a plurality of ends. We want recognition, gratitude, justice, fairness, loyalty, fidelity, respect, and well-being, yet these goods are not universally reconcilable. Honor and love are not the same. Justice and loyalty prove to be opposites. This does not make these goods any less desirable.

In sum, man is too many, his nature too complex, for single ideals and ends. The more we know men and women the more complex they become to us. The more we know our individual identity the more we know our many selves.

Ethics itself may foster pluralism. First, ethics is a science of debating the grounds of right and wrong. Where there is argumentation, different answers are stimulated. Second, ethics brings everything under reasoned examination, thereby raising inevitably more questions than solutions. Ethics, since the time it first appeared in the great religions and the earliest law codes, has questioned assumed values. With it was established the notion that the good life was a matter of reflection. Third, ethics as a tradition confronts us with the plurality of ends that inform human experience. Ethics, in this sense, is a collection of great thinkers, great questions, and great systems. Each gives a different insight. None are devoid of light. Therefore, to know ethics is to know how varied human thought and values are.

The convergence between ethics and a pluralistic view of the world suggests two additional insights: The first is that ethics' origins themselves are found in a changing and pluralistic world. Historically ethics came into existence when differing peoples encountered each other. Ethics, as embodied in the first philosophical systems of Greece or the religions of the near East, India, and China, came into existence when smaller groups and cultures were no longer autonomous. Ethics occurs where commercial, urban and political revolutions challenge traditional groups and values. Ethics can be understood to thrive where no one culture dominates, and individuals are compelled to face, and even seek to transcend, the cultural contradictions of an era.

Ethics, therefore, exists precisely when first assumptions are in doubt and the public world is involved in great change. Certainly the thinkers covered in this study would bear witness to this interpretation. They suffered ethics because they had to. Ethics thrives where the ethical community is felt to be most precarious. It survives where values are in radical contest.

The conditions for ethics are fully present in our times. The public life is involved in violent change. First premises are in disarray. No single power has clear authority. And only the most naive can nostalgically take ethical refuge in the old way; only the righteous can affirm that the future inevitably improves us.

For those who concern themselves with the ethical issues, there is consolation. Ethics proves to be a way to define essential boundaries.

As this insight consoles, so it pains. We cannot expect answers from ethics. Its individual insights can be uplifting. It can provide truths that join us to others. But ethics will not furnish the answers that will restore the best of tradition, set progress again on its promising path, help realize the greater good in the national and the international order. Studying ethics invariably proves to be a study in limits: It makes clear the limits of our knowledge, language, and ability to pursue a common good. To speak paradoxically, ethics is alive because of our era's crisis, but it is unable to give resolution to that crisis.

Perhaps the greater our hunger to see the good embodied, the less we judge ethics to be relevant. Ethics speaks of man without speaking for man. What it concludes, its prescriptions, are without force. It is religion that stirs men's and women's hearts, and politics provides a direction to our pursuit of earthly good.

Ethics, indeed, may fail the test of theory. It speaks of what ought to be, instead of what is. Surely it fails the test of action.

Ethics, however, does enlighten us. Its enlightenment is not an ascending revelation but, instead, a deepening descent into the shadowy realm of our responsibilities. And in the darkness only the fool denies the candle for its fragile light. Ethics is such a light.

NOTES

1. Christopher Lasch's *The Culture of Narcissism* (New York, 1978) and Richard Sennett's *The Fall of Public Man* (New York, 1977).

2. Reinhold Niebuhr titled one of his important works *Moral Man in Immoral Society* (New York, 1932). He was aware that the opposition he suggested was extreme.

3. Two works on the 1960s suggesting the awesome division youth felt between duty to nation and conscience are ed. Ronald Lora's *America in the '60s: Cultural Authorities in Transition* (New York, 1974) and ed. Massimo Teodori, *The New Left: A Documentary History* (New York, 1969). Also useful is Chapter V in Joseph Amato's forthcoming *Guilt and Gratitude* (Westport, Ct.).

4. The best argument for willingness to risk nuclear war is made in Karl Jaspers' *The Future of Mankind* (Chicago, 1963).

5. For a discussion of reciprocity see Chapter One of Amato, *Guilt and Gratitude*.

6. A recent attempt to establish a theory of justice upon contract and reciprocity is John Rawls' *Theory of Justice* (Cambridge, Mass., 1971).

7. To grasp the notion of *raison d'état*, reason of state, there is no substitute for Machiavelli's *The Prince* and *Discourses*, and Thucydides' *The History of the Peloponnesian Wars*.

8. Jacques Ellul, *The Political Illusion* (New York, 1967).

9. *Ibid.*, 187, 191.

10. For one example of the condition of contemporary man which breeds pessimism, see Kurt Glaser and Stefan Possony's *Victims of Politics: The State of Human Rights* (New York, 1979).

11. Claude Levi-Strauss, *The Origin of Table Manners* (New York, 1968), 508.

Bio-Bibliographies

ROUSSEAU

Jean Jacques Rousseau (1712-1778) was born in Geneva, Switzerland. His mother died shortly after his birth; his father, a watchmaker, did not provide him with a good education. At sixteen he set out wandering. He was taken in by his patroness, and later lover, Madame de Warens, who accounted for his initial conversion to Catholicism and deeply influenced his intellectual life.

In 1743, Rousseau arrived in Paris, hoping to make his fortune with a new system of musical notation. Although he did not succeed, he joined the circle of Diderot, editor of the great *Encyclopédie*, to which Rousseau contributed several pieces. At this time he began his lifelong relation with the servant and his common law wife, Thèrése Le Vasseur.

Rousseau began to write in earnest, and his life started that recurring cycle of winning new patrons by his genius and then breaking off relations with them because of his constant suspicions.

In 1749, Rousseau won the first prize in a contest staged by the Academy Dijon. To the official question, "has the progress in the sciences and arts contributed to the corruption or improvement of human conduct," Rousseau replied that civilization has corrupted man. In his 1754 *Discours sur l'origine de l'inégalite des hommes*, Rousseau attacked private property. He subsequently wrote *La Nouvelle Heloïse* (1761) – a sentimental novel based on his adulterous, but unconsecrated, love of Mme d'Houdetot. Then he wrote in 1762 an educational treatise, *Émile*, which stressed the development of what was best in the student's nature, and *The Social Contract*, which postulated a general will that morally joins and elevates its citizens. He last wrote his *Reveries du promeneur solitaire* (1774), *Confessions* (1766-1767), and *Dialogues: Rousseau juge de Jean-Jacques Rousseau* (1776). Each of these works expresses his search for self, place, and peace in the world.

Rousseau's writings won him praise, but also censure and condemnation came from all quarters, civil, ecclesiastical, and philosophical. His life seemed to be passed in a flight from real and imaginary enemies. This predecessor of Romanticism forever seemed to seek a home which ultimately only the grave could supply.

Rousseau died in 1778. He was buried near Paris. The revolutionists transferred his remains to the Panthéon in 1794.

For works about Rousseau, see Irving Babbitt's *Rousseau and Romanticism* (New York, 1919), Ernst Cassirer's *The Question of Jean-Jacques Rousseau* (Bloomington, Indiana, 1963), Lester G. Crocker's *Jean-Jacques Rousseau* (2 vols, New York, 1973), Jean Guéhenno's *Jean-Jacques Rousseau* (Columbia, 1966), Matthew Josephson's *Jean-Jacques Rousseau* (New York, 1970), Jacques Maritain's *Three Reformers: Luther, Descartes, Rousseau* (New York, 1928).

Additionally for Rousseau, see Louis Althusser's *Politics and History: Montesquieu, Rousseau, Hegel and Marx* (New York, 1978), David Cameron's *The Social Thought of Rousseau and Burke* (Toronto, 1973), and Ronald Grimsley's *The Philosophy of Rousseau* (New York, 1973).

KARL MARX

Karl Marx (1818-1883) was the chief theorist of modern socialism and communism. His life-long intellectual goal was to grasp the fundamental forces which moved history and to develop the workers party which would lead to a new social order.

Marx was born in Treves, the second of seven children. For many generations the male forebears on both sides of his family had been rabbis in Holland and Germany. His father was a well-to-do lawyer.

Marx himself studied law at Bonn and Berlin. Eventually, however, his interests shifted to philosophy in which he received a Ph.D. at Jena, in 1841. Marx was prominent among the young Hegelians, those younger German thinkers who sought to transform the work of Hegel to serve the supposed timely needs of their own generation.

In 1842, Marx became editor of the *Rheinische Zeitung*. Its call for radical reforms led to its suppression in 1843. Marx fled to Paris. There he and Friedrich Engels met, beginning a life-long collaboration, perhaps the most famous in all history. Marx also there entered into contract with the most advanced French social thinkers. Ultimately in critical dialogue with them, he articulated a distinct body of radical social theory.

He joined the Communist League and, with Engels, wrote the famous *Communist Manifesto*. He preached the historical inevitability of class struggle and argued that the forthcoming struggle between the proletariat and capitalist classes was the decisive struggle for a new humanity.

Again in exile, after the failure of the 1848 revolutions, Marx took up permanent residence in London in 1849. There he lived in poverty as he continued his dedication to writing his magnum opus, *Das Kapital:* a definition of capitalist economics and economic value. His other journalistic and scholarly writings covered a vast array of subjects, which included such topics as the Crimean War, agriculture, the Russian peasantry, and mathematics.

Marx's dedication to writing did not exclude attempts to change society by direct political action. In 1864 he helped to found the First International Working Men's Association—and throughout its ten year existence, Marx never ceased to conspire to assure the primacy of his socialism over the followers of anarchist Bakunin and democratic nationalist Mazzini. Marx destroyed the First International, rather than allow it to pass into the wrong hands. Believing that the 1871 rising of the Paris Commune against France's German conquerors and their puppet authorities constituted a true class revolution, Marx issued the call for revolution.

After his wife's death in 1881 Marx's health steadily deteriorated until his death in 1883. His ideas, however, did not die. Thanks especially to Engels, Marxism became by the 1890s the dominant radical doctrine of the world.

For the formation of Marx, useful are Karl Löwith, *From Hegel to Nietzsche. The Revolution in Nineteenth-Century Thought*, (New York, 1964), Sidney Hook, *From Hegel to Marx* (Ann Arbor, 1962), Jean Hyppolite's *Studies on Marx and Hegel* (New York, 1969), Shlomo Avineri's *The Social and Political Thought of Karl Marx* (Cambridge, England, 1968). A convenient collection of young Marx's writing is eds. Loyd Easton and Kurt Guddat's *The Writings of the Young Marx on Philosophy and Society* (Garden City, N.Y., 1967). Among generally useful works on Marx are Isaiah Berlin's *Karl Marx* (Oxford, 1939), John H. Jackson's *Marx, Proudhon, and European Socialism* (New York, 1962), George Lichtheim's *Marxism: An Historical and Critical Study* (New York, 1961), Tucker's *Philosophy and Myth in Karl Marx* (Cambridge, Mass., 1961).

Also on Marx see David McLellan's *Karl Marx* (New York, 1976) and Melvin Rader's *Marx's Interpretation of History* (New York, 1979).

DOSTOEVSKY

Feodor Dostoevsky, 1821-1881, was born and raised in Moscow by Russian Orthodox parents. His father was a military surgeon who was slain by his own serfs. Dostoevsky attended military engineering school in St. Petersburg and, upon graduation, he entered government service as a draftsman. He soon abandoned this career for writing. He associated himself with Belinski's circle, the most advanced literary circle in Russia.

His first published work, *Poor Folk*, 1846, brought him wide recognition. It revealed his characteristic compassion for the downtrodden. His second piece *The Double*, also published in 1846, though not well received, nevertheless shows the profound insight into human nature that characterizes his later works.

Dostoevsky's involvement with a group of radical utopians, inspired by French thinkers, led to his arrest and a death sentence. The death sentence was commuted by the Tsar moments before his execution. During his four years of hard labor in Siberia he developed chronic epilepsy, which plagued him for the rest of his life.

After ten years in Siberia, Dostoevsky was allowed to return to St. Petersburg. Thence begins the period of his great writings: *The Insulted and the Injured*, 1861; *Notes From The Underground*, 1864; *Crime and Punishment*, 1866; *The Idiot*, 1869; *The Possessed*, 1871-1872; *A Raw Youth*, 1875; and his greatest work of all, *The Brothers Karamazov*, 1879-1880.

His success as a writer in no way meant an easy life. Dostoevsky and his family were always on the edge of poverty due to his meager income and his passion for gambling. He always wrote under the twin pressures of poverty and deadlines. He constantly moved about in Western Europe. Bitterness, anger, remorse, and other powerful emotions were his constant companions.

The perfect devotion of his second wife, Anna Grigoryevna Snitkina, gave his life what order it had. He died in 1881, never escaping from the psychological agonies of guilt, shame, and evil, which were the very source of his novels.

For useful guides to Dostoevsky, see Nicholas Berdyaev's *Dostoevsky* (Cleveland, 1957), Donald Fanger's *Dostoevsky and Romantic Realism* (Cambridge, Mass., 1965), Joseph Frank's *The Seeds of Revolt* (Princeton, 1976), Vyacheslav Ivanov's *A Study in Dostoevsky* (New York, 1963), and David Magarshack's *Dostoevsky* (Princeton, 1967).

Additionally for Dostoevsky, see Anna Dostoevsky, *Dostoevsky, Reminiscences* (New York, 1977), Ronald Hingley's *Dostoevsky: His Life and Work* (New York, 1978), and George Panichas' *Burden of Vision* (Grand Rapids, Michigan, 1977).

FRIEDRICH NIETZSCHE

Friedrich Wilhelm Nietzsche, 1844-1900, born in Röcken, Prussia, was the son of a Lutheran minister. He was brought up in a household of five women. He studied classical philology at the universities of Bonn and Leipzig.

He served as a medical aide during the Franco-Prussian War of 1870. As a teacher at the University of Basel in Switzerland, Nietzsche came under the influence of historian Jacob Burckhardt. Nietzsche shared Burckhardt's pessimism regarding the modern age and turned Burckhardt's notion that a new culture was required for the resurgence of man into a personal mission.

Though once friendly with composer Richard Wagner, Nietzsche broke with him, denouncing the vulgar, romantic nationalism of his music. His resignation from the University of Basel in 1879, forced by nervous disturbances and eye trouble, began a long decade marked by profound loneliness and great creation.

In 1889, after Burckhardt and others received a succession of insane letters from Nietzsche, friends were sent to Turin to bring him home. He lived the last decade of his life under the care of his mother and sister. He never regained his sanity. He died in 1900 a shell of a man.

He had made himself a crucible of the modern world and with each succeeding decade his influence upon Western intellectual life has grown.

For works by Nietzsche, see *Complete Works*, ed. by Oscar Levy, (New York, 1964), *The Philosophy of Nietzsche* (New York, 1937), *The Portable Nietzsche* (New York, 1954), *The Birth of Tragedy and The Genealogy of Morals* (New York, 1967), *Thus Spake Zarathustra* (New York, 1961), *Beyond Good and Evil* (New York, 1966), and *The Will to Power*, (New York, 1967).

For works on Nietzsche, see Frederick Copleston's *Friedrich Nietzsche*(New York, 1975), Karl Jaspers' *Nietzsche and Christianity* (New York, 1961), Walter Kaufmann's *Nietzsche* (Princeton, 1968), Karl Löwith's *From Hegel to Nietzsche* (New York, 1964), Lev Shestov's *Dostoevsky, Tolstoy and Nietzsche* (Columbus, 1970), and Stefan Zweig's "A One-Man Drama," *Master Builders* (New York, 1939), 443-530.

Also on Nietzsche, see R. J. Hollingdale's *Nietzsche* (Boston, 1973), and J. P. Stern's *Nietzsche* (New York, 1979).

HENRY ADAMS

Henry Adams (1838-1918) was an historian. Born in Quincy, near Boston, Adams was the son of Charles Francis Adams, important Republican politician, ambassador, and writer, the grandson of John Quincy Adams, sixth president of the United States, and great grandson of John Adams, second president of the United States. If there had been such a thing as the American aristocracy, Henry Adams would have been a member of it.

Adams studied at Harvard. Upon graduation in 1858, in accord with the fashion of the era, he went to study in Germany. He also traveled widely in Europe, trying his hand at journalism.

He served as under-secretary for his father, who held the all-important post of United States minister to Britain during the Civil War. This was a source of Adams' understanding of international politics. After the Civil War, Adams sought a career as a journalist in Grant's Washington. This soured his belief in democracy.

Gratefully, Adams accepted a post as a medievalist at Harvard. During his seven year stint at Harvard (1870-1877), Adams was considered to be an excellent teacher. He left Harvard to edit the influential *North American Review*. There he produced important articles on contemporary financial and scientific matters.

In 1872 he married Marian Hooper. In 1877 they settled in Washington, where they were regular hosts to "the best of Europe and America." During that period Adams did his most productive research and writing. He published, under a pseudonym, two satirical novels, *Democracy* (1879) and *Esther* (1884). Both works focused on the agonies of a good woman caught in the evils and corruption of a male world. During this period Adams also was at work on his monumental study of the Jeffersonian and Madison presidencies. His nine volume *History of the United States of America from 1801 to 1817* (published 1889 to 1891) is one of the major achievements of American historical writing. No doubt it accounted for his election to be president of the American Historical Association.

Adams' pessimism turned cosmic with the suicide of his wife in 1885. He abandoned formal history. He began a series of restless journeys in space and mind to find the world he had been cheated out of. His conclusion was vividly stated in his *Education*: the forces of the modern world were not to be understood or controlled. Democratic, technological, and scientific revolutions would make man's future despite man.

Adams died in Washington in 1918. He had lived a long life, each year of which carried him a step further away from the aristocrat republic of his forefathers, into the alien world of mass democracy.

Two useful works on Adams are Ernest Samuel's 3 vol. *Henry Adams* (Cambridge, Mass., 1948-1964), and Elizabeth Stevenson's *Henry Adams* (New York, 1955).

Recent works on Henry Adams include Ferman Bishop's *Henry Adams* (Boston, 1979) and John Rowe's *Henry Adams and Henry James:*

The Emergence of a Modern Consciousness (Ithaca, New York, 1976).

EMMANUEL MOUNIER

Emmanuel Mounier was born in 1905. He died prematurely of a heart attack in 1950. He gave his adult life over to two main projects, the editing of the progressive and influential Catholic journal *Esprit* and the articulation of the doctrine *Personalism*.

Mounier was born into a middle class family. He never seriously questioned his attachment to the Church. After a difficult period of indecision about his career, Mounier made his choice for philosophy and teaching. And like most young promising French intellectuals, his career led from the outlying regions of France to Paris, from the University of Grenoble to the *École Normale*.

Though passing his examinations from the *École Normale* with high honors, he never completed his doctorate. His commitment to the service of Catholicism and his attempt to relate it to the crisis of his era led him, along with his contemporary Georges Izard, to found *Esprit*. Under the intellectual influences of Charles Péguy, Henri Bergson, Jacques Chevalier, Jacques Maritain, and Nicholas Berdyaev, Mounier did not hesitate to presume to speak for his generation and humanity.

Married, with three children, and teaching in Belgium, Mounier had little time for anything other than *Esprit* and his writing. Even with the coming of the Second World War and France's defeat and occupation by Germany, Mounier's life still was his teaching and writing. However, finding it impossible to teach and to keep *Esprit* alive under the collaborationist Vichy régime, Mounier lent his active support to the Resistance.

In the post-war, Mounier refounded *Esprit* with a younger generation of Catholic and Protestant thinkers. His talk about a new civilization became virtually non-existent; his search for what could be called a democratic, Christian socialism became explicit.

When he died in 1950 his accomplishments were *Personalism* and *Esprit*. He had helped to teach two generations of French intellectuals and young thinkers throughout Europe and Latin America that Catholicism no longer needed to mean indifference or reaction.

For the most economical introduction to Mounier, see his 1950 *Personalism* (Notre Dame, 1970), as well as Joseph Amato's *Mounier and Maritain: A French Catholic Understanding of the Modern World* (University, Ala., 1975).

For a forthcoming addition to the study of Mounier, see John

Hellman's *Emmanuel Mounier and the New Catholic Left, 1930 to 1950* (Toronto, 1982).

ALBERT CAMUS

Albert Camus (1913-1960) was a French essayist, playwright, and novelist. Camus was born in Mondovi, Algiers, into an illiterate working class family. His father was killed on the Western Front in 1914. Camus was brought up by his mother and grandmother in the slums of Algiers.

Throughout his writings Camus depicted Algiers to be the land of light, sand, and sea, the habitat of sensual, embodied man. That man represents, for Camus, all that is enduring and worthwhile about humanity.

Camus' attachment to the theatre started while at the University of Algiers. He acted in, adapted, and directed plays. Though active in left wing movements in the 1930s, Camus' dedication was to the theatre and writing. In 1939, Camus went to Paris as a journalist.

During the Second World War Camus committed himself to the French Resistance. He was the principal editor of the chief resistance publication, *Combat*. He wrote a steady stream of articles for it. Also during the war he published *The Myth of Sisyphus*, a collection of essays, that declared the fundamental theme of Camus' philosophy: the need to seek meaning in a meaningless world.

From then on Camus sought the first principles of being human and being part of the human community in a world afflicted by madness and cruelty. This search, which characterized his plays and humanistic essays (esp. *The Rebel*), increasingly led Camus to be critical of Marxism. His criticism of Marxism alienated him from the French left, as did his effort to find a middle position on the decolonization of Algiers.

Camus won the Nobel Prize in literature in 1957. To the shock of the educated West, Camus died in an auto wreck in 1960.

A few useful introductions to Camus include Richard Akeroyd's *The Spiritual Quest of Albert Camus* (Tuscaloosa, Ala., 1976), Germaine Brée's *Camus and Sartre* (New York, 1972), Herbert Lottman's *Albert Camus: A Biography* (Garden City, New York, 1979), and Conor Cruise O'Brien's *Albert Camus of Europe and Africa* (New York, 1970).

Also on Camus, see Maurice Friedman *Problematic Rebel: Melville, Dostoevsky, Kafka, Camus* (Chicago, 1970), and Herbert Lottman's *Albert Camus* (New York, 1979).

JEAN-PAUL SARTRE

Jean-Paul Sartre, 1905-1980, is known as France's, if not the world's premier intellectual of the twentieth century. Sartre was a playwright, novelist, essayist, and intellectual biographer. Sartre was born into an upper class French family, intermarried with the famous Schweitzer family. With the death of his father, the young Sartre and his mother went to live with his sober, dominant, grandfather Schweitzer. Of his isolated childhood in the Schweitzer household, Sartre said, "Books were my companions."

The themes of isolation and defiance were continuous throughout his life. His pride was always in his defiance of the conventional life of the bourgeois. Children, family, religion – none ever had a place in the mature Sartre's life. Sartre always lived by and for his thought. His literary heroes were isolated men (Baudelaire, Genet, and Flaubert). The philosophical systems he preferred were those that conceived of men and women to exist in a mute, alien universe. As much as any other, Sartre wears the title of the founder of existentialism. In its name he preached a doctrine of man as totally free.

After graduating from the *École Normale* and studying philosophy in Germany in the early 1930s, Sartre's sole dedication became being a great writer. His first novel, *Nausea* (1938), was followed by *Intimacy* (1939), a collection of short stories.

Sartre served in the army during World War II. He was taken prisoner, escaped, and became a leader in the Resistance. During the occupation, he wrote his first plays, *The Flies* (1943) and *No Exit* (1944), and the monumental treatise in philosophy, *Being and Nothingness* (1943). The Resistance experience taught Sartre the necessity of full political commitment. With Merleau-Ponty, Sartre founded the influential activist journal, *Les temps moderns*. Also, his notion of commitment increasingly led Sartre in the direction of Marxism. On most issues – be it sympathy to Russia or resistance to the Americanization of Europe, the struggle against French colonial rule of Algiers in the 1950s or American imperialism in Vietnam in the 1960s – Sartre led the causes of the radical left in France. In the wake of the French crisis of 1968, which toppled the De Gaulle régime, Sartre threw his full support to the young Maoist extremists.

Sartre was always a man of extremes. He pushed his literary searches, his philosophical principles, as well as his conception of individual and collective man, to extremes. He mirrored and exaggerated this century's excessive rationalism, despair, godlessness, egoism, and despairing humanism.

In 1964 he declined the Nobel Prize in Literature on the grounds that such recognition lends too much importance to a writer's influence. When he died in 1980, it was clear that he was the West's most prominent intellectual.

For introductory guides to Sartre see Ronald Aronson's *Jean-Paul Sartre* (London, 1980), Germaine Brée's *Camus and Sartre* (New York, 1972), Thomas Molnar's *Sartre* (New York, 1968), and ed. Mary Warnock's *Sartre: A Collection of Critical Essays* (Garden City, N.Y., 1971).

Additionally for Sartre, see Pietro Chiodi's *Sartre and Marxism* (New York, 1976), Arthur Danto's *Jean-Paul Sartre* (New York, 1975), and George Stack's *Sartre's Philosophy of Social Existence* (Hamden, Connecticut, 1978).

Index of Names

Adams, Brooks, 73, 75
Adams, Charles Francis, 75, 76, 123, 124
Adams, Henry, 2-3, 68, 71-86, 87, 114, 116, 123-5
Adams, Louisa, 77
Adams, Marian Hooper, 81-2, 124
Addams, Jane, 79
Agassiz, Alexander, 78
Agassiz, Louis, 78

Babbit, Irving, 21
Bakunin, Mikhail, 50, 121
Baudelaire, Charles, 101, 104-5, 127
Belinski, Vissarion, 122
Bentham, Jeremy, 12
Berdyaev, Nicholas, 125
Bergson, Henri, 125
Blum, Léon, 92
Burckhardt, Jacob, 65-6, 68, 70, 123

Camerons, James and Elizabeth, 82
Camus, Albert, 2-3, 85, 95-100, 106, 107-8, 111, 115, 126
Cassirer, Ernst, 20
Chevalier, Jacques, 125
Child, Francis, 78
Comte, Auguste, 27, 73

De Gaulle, Charles, 92
Diderot, Denis, 13, 119
Dostoevsky, Feodor, 2-3, 30, 33, 35-51, 53, 64, 65, 80, 83, 88, 96, 98, 101, 108, 111, 114, 116, 121-2

Dumas, Alexandre, 78
Durkheim, Émile, 71

Ellul, Jacques, 114
Engels, Friedrich, 120-1

Fanon, Frantz, 105
Feuerbach, Ludwig, 28, 31
Fiske, John, 78
Flaubert, Gustave, 127
Foucault, Michel, 107
Freud, Sigmund, 49, 88

Gast, Peter, 65
Genet, Jean, 101, 127
Gide, André, 105, 108
Goethe, Johann Wolfgang von, 56-7, 67
Grant, Ulysses, 76-7
Gurney, Ephraim, 78

Halévy, Élie, 12
Harte, Bret, 79
Hauser, Arnold, 22
Hay, John, 79, 82
Hegel, Georg Wilhelm Friedrich, 27-8, 33, 37, 98, 99, 120
Heidegger, Martin, 100
Herzen, Alexander, 50-1
Hitler, Adolph, 87, 99
Houdetot, Elisabeth, madame de, 16, 119
Hume, David, 14, 17
Husserl, Edmund, 100

Izard, Georges, 125

130 / Index of Names

James, Henry, 79
James, William, 78
Jung, Carl, 88

Kant, Immanuel, 11
Kierkegaard, Søren, 64
King, Clarence, 79, 82

La Farge, John, 79
Lasch, Christopher, 111
La Rochefoucauld, François,
    duc de, 64
Lautréamont, Isidore, comte de, 98
Le Vasseur, Thérèse, 119
Lévi-Strauss, Claude, 114
Lowell, James Russell, 78
Löwith, Karl, 29

Mann, Thomas, 86
Maritain, Jacques, 20-1, 125
Marx, Karl, 2-3, 25-34, 35, 79,
    88, 89, 92, 98, 99, 111, 120-1
Mazzini, Giuseppe, 26, 121
Merleau-Ponty, Maurice, 100,
    109, 127
Michelet, Jules, 26
Montaigne, Michel, 108
Mounier, Emmanuel, 2-3, 85-94,
    97, 111, 115, 125-6
Mumford, Lewis, 85

Nicholas I, tsar, 35-6, 46
Nietzsche, Friedrich, 2-3, 53-70,
    71-2, 82, 85, 88, 89, 93, 96, 98,
    99, 114, 116, 122-3
Nizan, Paul, 101

Overbeck, Franz, 66

Pascal, Blaise, 64, 108, 116
Peyre, Henri, 20
Péguy, Charles, 92, 125
Phillips, William, 79

Richardson, H. H., 79
Rousseau, Jean-Jacques, 2-3,
    11-23, 66-7, 98, 105, 106, 111,
    119-20

Sade, Donatien, comte de, 98
Saint-Simon, Claude Henri,
    comte de, 26, 34
Sartre, Jean-Paul, 2-3, 85, 92, 95,
    96, 99-110, 111, 115, 116, 127-8
Schweitzer, Charles, 103, 127
Scott, Walter, 78
Sennett, Richard, 111
Snitkina, Anna Grigoryevna, 122
Socrates, 54, 55
Strindberg, Johan August, 65

Tolstoi, Leo, Count, 58

Verga, Giuseppe, 7
Voltaire, François Arouet de, 64,
    67

Wagner, Richard, 65, 123
Warren, Louise-Eléonore,
    madame de, 16, 119
Weber, Max, 71

About the Author

Joseph A. Amato is a Professor of History at Southwest State University in Marshall, Minnesota. He was born in 1938 in Detroit, Michigan, and received his B.A. from the University of Michigan in 1960, M.A. from the University of Laval in Quebec in 1963, and his Ph.D. from the University of Rochester in 1970. His doctoral dissertation on modern French Catholic thought was published by the University of Alabama Press under the title *Mounier and Maritain: A French Catholic Understanding of the Modern World* (1975).

After teaching at the University of New York, Binghamton, and the University of California, Riverside, he came to Southwest State in 1969. Since then, along with his wife and four children, he has lived in southwestern Minnesota, taking interests in a variety of local civic matters concerning rural life, labor, and the environment, as well as matters of college governance and teacher unionization. Much of the spirit and form of his activism are derived from what he learned in the 1960s from the Catholic Worker and war protest movements.

Recently Amato has turned his attention to writing. He has written over thirty book reviews, articles on family, ethnicity, anarchism, as well as the Sicilian social reformer Danilo Dolci, and the striking bank women of Willmar, Minnesota. He recently published for the American Farm Project, a project sponsored by the National Endowment for the Humanities, a set of reflective essays on the countryside, *Countryside, Mirror of Ourselves*. A second edition has been recently published by his own press, Venti Amati.

Amato's major forthcoming work is *Guilt and Gratitude, A Study of the Origins of Contemporary Conscience* (Greenwood Press, 1982). He is presently at work on books on the subjects of pain and intimacy. He also is writing a book of personal reflections.